Theresa
wish.

Erick Connell
Alaska 2010

Beyond the Northern Horizon

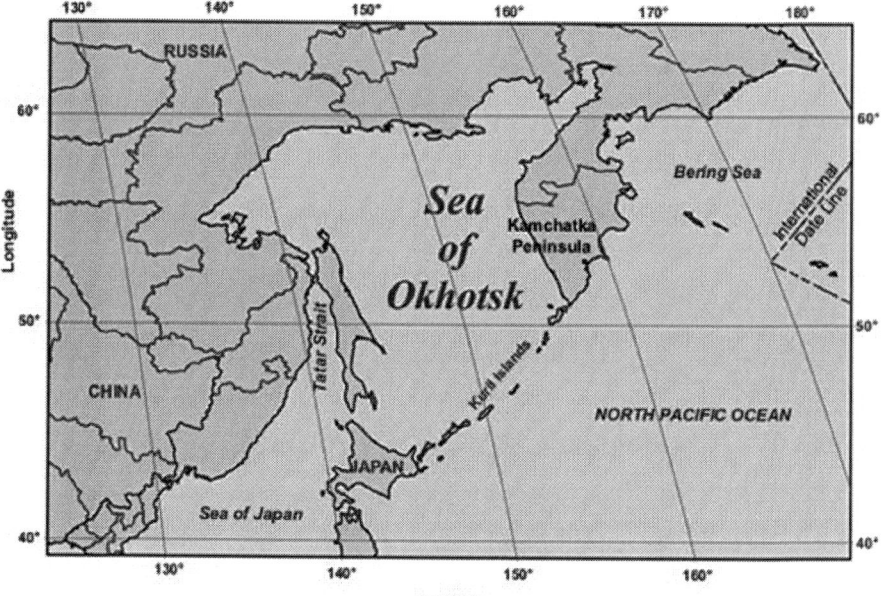

Beyond the Northern Horizon

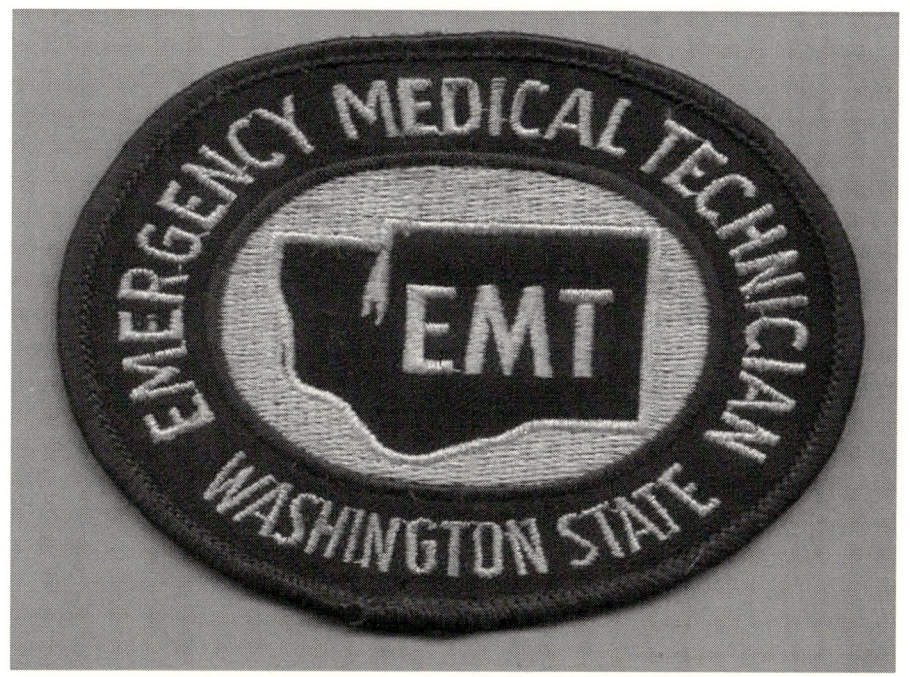

Erick Connell

Copyright © 2010 by Erick Connell.

Library of Congress Control Number: 2010904454
ISBN: Hardcover 978-1-4500-5707-3
Softcover 978-1-4500-5706-6
E-book 978-1-4500-4699-2

All rights reserved. No part of this book may be reproduced or transmitted in any form or by any means, electronic or mechanical, including photocopying, recording, or by any information storage and retrieval system, without permission in writing from the copyright owner.

This book was printed in the United States of America.

To order additional copies of this book, contact:
Xlibris Corporation
1-888-795-4274
www.Xlibris.com
Orders@Xlibris.com
78930

Contents

I.	Casualty of the wind	9
II.	Ocean Planet	17
III.	Naming the Void	24
IV.	The Beginning	34
V.	M/V Royal Enterprise	38
VI.	A fist full of Dynamite	44
VII.	In Bering's Wake	55
VIII.	The Wave	69
IX.	Jumping Ship	78
X.	Transformation	92
XI.	Homeward Bound	101
XII.	The End or the Beginning	108
XIII.	Voyages of the Northern Jaeger 1991-1996	114
XIV.	Return to Kamchatka	143
XV.	The Floating Town	159
XVI.	Bombs Away	168
XVII.	The Labyrinth Disease and the Heart	175
XVIII.	An Arm and a Leg	187
XIX.	End of an Era 1996	210

Epilogue 215
Dedication 219
About the Author 221

Acknowledgments

I would like to acknowledge those reference sources which were helpful in my research. Particularly in writing the chapter "Naming the Void," the story on the Bering Expedition, I relied on Stephen Haycox's *Alaska: An American Colony* published by the University of Washington Press in 2002. I am grateful for Web sites such as ScienceDaily and others featuring the biography of Vitus Bering and information on the Marianas Trench, USS *Trieste*, Alaskan pollock, the Aleutian Islands, and the Kamchatka Peninsula.

Ships are safe in harbor, but that's not what ships are built for.

—John A. Shedd

Chapter 1

Casualty of the wind

Trawler on the Bering Sea

It was two in the morning. I hadn't been able to sleep all night due to the storm raging outside. I was startled by a loud pounding on my cabin door, knowing immediately it could be for only one thing that time of the morning.

A head popped out from around the door saying, "Doc, you're needed down in the engine room. Gary's been hurt."

Rising from my bunk, I asked, "Is it bad?"

"It's pretty bad, Doc. You'd better hurry." As fast as the messenger had appeared, he was gone, leaving me to stumble out of my bunk to get dressed.

The ship rocked violently, listing precariously to starboard, forcing me to struggle to keep my balance. As I continued to get dressed as fast as I could, I felt the bow of the ship plunge down into the valley between two mountainous waves. At the bottom, the bow knifed down below the surface; then in slow motion, the ship began to struggle back up out from under the tons of water that conspired to send her to a watery grave.

Gaining her buoyancy, she began to rise up onto the other side of the wave; as she did, she threw off the massive volume of water that had just tried to take her down in an explosion of white water and spray.

I staggered over to the porthole, drawn to witness the tempest that howled outside. A screaming wind tore the tops of forty-foot waves, shredding the green water into a white spray, then into a mist that vaporized into the inky blackness. The primal scene I was witnessing was mesmerizing, and it was difficult to pull myself away.

I finished dressing and grabbed my trauma bag and began to make my way down the hallway to the engine room all the while being tossed about from bulkhead to bulkhead as the ship continued her fight to stay afloat. In the dull fluorescent light of the engine room, I made out several men leaning over someone lying next to one of the massive diesel engines.

The sound of the engines was deafening; someone handed me a set of headphone ear protectors, which I put on eagerly. I gently pushed my way past the men leaning over Gary. I kneeled down next to him. He looked at me with a frightened expression, holding a greasy rag over the right side of face. His eyes met mine, looking for my reaction.

I slowly moved the rag away from his face to get a look at his injury, careful not to make any expression that might upset him. His right cheek from the top of his lip up diagonally to near the bottom of his right ear was laid open with a jagged gash. For just an instant,

I caught a glimpse of white cheekbone before it was obscured when blood immediately began to flow as the pressure to the wound was released. I gently placed Gary's hand holding the greasy blood-soaked rag back over the wound, explaining to him to keep firm pressure on the wound and that he'd be fine.

Standing up, I leaned over to the nearest engineer and put my mouth next to his ear. "What happened?" I yelled, straining to be heard over the roar of the engines.

He produced an eighteen-inch, five-pound pipe wrench and pointed up to the top of an engine. He made a motion with the sweep of his hand indicating that the wrench had fallen off the top of the engine and struck Gary in the face at a height of about eight feet.

I motioned to the other guys gathered round to help get him moved topside to the cabin I used as an infirmary. As we struggled to get him up the several flight of stairs to the deck above, I was wondering how I was going to pull this off. By now I had become good at suturing cuts on fingers, hands, and extremities but had never sutured someone's face before and never in this kind of weather. I wasn't sure I could do it in such a fierce storm as this.

The only thing I knew for sure at that moment was I had to try. On the way up, I asked if someone would go wake up Maria. One of the few women on the ship, she worked in the galley and over the years had become my extra pair of hands when I needed them. I didn't know then that on that night I'd need them more than ever.

By that time, it was hard to remain standing in one spot as the ship lurched sharply and violently as huge waves pounded her from every direction. As we finally made it to the infirmary, I instructed those aiding Gary to lay him in one of the bunks and hold on to him to keep him from falling out onto the floor.

The ship listed hard to port over to a forty-five-degree angle as all of us found something bolted down to hang on to. As I opened the cabinet to get out my equipment, the contents flew out across the room, rolling across the deck to the far side of the room and then back again as the ship listed forty-five degrees to the starboard.

As Gary patiently watched from the bunk, I scurried on my hands and knees around the room trying to retrieve my instruments all the while reassuring him everything was going to be fine. About that time Maria arrived and began to help, both of us on the floor then doing our best to gather everything rolling around. Just then the ship's phone began to ring.

"For God's sake, what now?" I muttered to myself as I answered the phone. "This is the infirmary. What do you want?" I was growing irritated and impatient at all the delays. To my surprise, it was the captain. "Sorry, Captain, I didn't know it was you."

"No problem, Doc. How's it going down there?"

"It's not," I shot back. "I can't get anything done in these seas. Gary is hurt pretty bad. It's a face wound, and I can't sew him up under these conditions."

"Well, I can change course for a while which will give you a smoother ride, but only for a half hour or so. Can you finish in that amount of time?" he asked.

My mind went blank for a second, kind of like a pinball machine on tilt. I had no idea if I could even sew him up let alone how long it would take. "Ah, yeah, sure, I'll have to. Thanks," I responded.

"Call me as soon as you finish, and hold on tight. This will be a rough turn." Then he hung up.

I hung up the phone and turned to everyone in the room. "Brace yourselves. We're changing course."

A moment later, I could feel the ship begin to strain as it responded to the rudder. I was taken by surprise as the distant sounds of unknown items began crashing to the deck in other compartments. The ship shuddered in response to a forty-foot wave slamming into her side. As the ship began to list over on her side, it simultaneously lifted its bow high out of the water and plunged down hard into the churning sea below.

The effect was like a truck slamming on its brakes at 50 mph, then instantly flooring the gas pedal, and accelerating off a cliff. *Wow*! What a wild ride.

We all held on for dear life. After several minutes, things began to calm down; the ship slowly stabilized, and the violent motion we had been experiencing moments before subsided. Although it was still rough, it was a little better. I knew this was my cue. I had thirty minutes to finish, starting that moment.

Maria and I quickly gathered up the equipment off the floor. I asked one of the engineers to hold everything on the small table I had set next to the bunk the best he could. I handed Maria a flashlight, instructing her to keep the light focused on the needle and thread as I made passes with the needle through Gary's skin.

There are different gauges of needles and thread, depending on the size and location of the cut being sewn closed. Let's say there's a large, wide laceration on the upper leg in the thigh area; a heavy-gauge needle and thick thread would then be used. The needle looks like a fishhook. In this case, it would need a large fishhook, the kind used to catch a large bass or trout. The thread would be thick like string and black in color, very easy to see as well as handle and tie knots. These work great for those kinds of wounds where there are thick, tough skin tissue to pierce, needing strong thread to pull the two sides of the cut back together. In those cases, there's no worry about scarring.

The gauges progressively become smaller and finer in diameter as the wounds they're used for become smaller and in more sensitive locations on the body until one gets to the finest gauge with a tiny hooked needle and thread resembling a spiderweb.

The finest gauge was what I was going to use that night, with the face being one of the most sensitive areas of the body where the skin is thin. Also I was very concerned about the effects of scarring on the face, for obvious reasons. It would be a very delicate procedure even in the most ideal circumstances and one I'd never done before.

In the dim fluorescent lighting used on board the ship, this gauge thread would be virtually invisible to the eye unless another light source such as a flashlight was used. Everything I used in this procedure had to be sterilized with alcohol. The most important consideration was postinfection to the wound, a very serious development that can have more serious consequences than the wound itself.

So I needed to clean the wound extremely well. Next I needed to numb the wound so I could stick a needle through Gary's face. This required using a syringe to inject the drug lidocaine. As the name implies, it is a derivative of cocaine and is used to numb the tissue around the wound.

It took a half-dozen or more injections in various locations in and around the wound to ensure that there was no feeling in that area. Then I proceeded to sew the wound closed, trying to ensure the minimum amount of scarring or deformity to the face as possible—all these while pitching and rolling in a gale.

As the clock ticked and everyone focused intently on my every move, the pressure was overwhelming. Above all, I needed to look like I knew what I was doing even though I didn't. As I hovered over Gary with a needle and syringe inches from his face, the ship listed hard to port then to starboard all the while rising up one side of a wave and then plunging down the other side.

Gary looked at me with a look I'd call terror. With my calmest and most professional voice, I softly reassured him everything would be fine and was under control. To my amazement, he seemed to believe me, and I could see his muscles relax as he settled back into the bunk.

I focused my attention on the motion of the ship, trying to sense any rhyme or rhythm to its movements as I began to inject the needle and the drug around his wound. Occasionally one of the vials of lidocaine or my forceps would fly off the table and slide across the floor, and one of the onlookers would chase it down and bring it back to the table. Very carefully and slowly, I began to take the fine needle and pierce his skin first through one side of the laceration then the other, drawing the two sides of his wound together gently just until they met. Then moving up the laceration, I repeated the process.

Every so often, the ship would make a sudden lurch to one side or the other, and I would freeze immediately using my arms and hands like shock absorbers to keep from plunging the needle into Gary's face or eyes. I was sweating heavily, and beads of sweat strung my eyes as I tried to say focused on the invisible silklike thread. Maria used a towel to wipe the sweat away with one hand while holding the flashlight on the thread with the other. Finally after what seemed hours, the last stitch was tied, and the thread cut. I was finished.

I gave the wound one last swipe with an alcohol swab and immediately stood to my feet and went to the phone to call the wheelhouse. "All finished," I said as the captain answered the phone.

"Good work," he replied then said, "hold on, I'm changing course," and hung up. Everyone knew what to expect and scurried to grab hold of something stable as we began to feel the ship turn. Our wild ride began anew as the captain steadied the ship on our original course.

"How do I look, Doc?" Gary finally asked.

"I think it looks good," I replied. I looked over to the others in the room and asked them, "What do you guys think?"

To my relief, the verdict was unanimous. "It looks really good, Doc. Great job." The more I had a chance to look at the stitched wound, the more pleased I was with the results.

Someone handed Gary a mirror. He looked at himself for several moments; the room fell silent with anticipation. Finally a smile grew across his face as he turned his head toward me. "Great job, Doc. It looks really good, man. Thanks." It was then that I felt a wave of utter emotional and physical exhaustion wash over me. I'd done it.

The relief of success was a wonderful feeling quickly replaced with the realization that I was utterly exhausted. I would start my next twelve-hour shift in a few short hours, and I had already been awake for twenty-one hours. I left Maria to finish cleaning up and putting the equipment away. I made sure Gary was comfortable; for him, this voyage was over. Like the wounded on a battlefield, he would be transferred to a ship inbound for Dutch Harbor. There he'd be flown to Anchorage seven hundred miles east and taken to a hospital.

I then made my way to my cabin, dropped my trauma bag on the floor, took off my boots, and collapsed into my bunk. Although the storm still raged outside and the ship was still locked in her primal battle with the sea, within seconds I was fast asleep. Another day as a medic in the Bering Sea was over.

No one would have ever crossed the ocean if they could have gotten off the ship in a storm.

—Unknown

Chapter 2

Ocean Planet

Coast Guard Cutter *Northwind*, 1975

Undeniably the Bering Sea is one of the most remote and least thought-of regions on Earth. To this day and forevermore, this part of the world will remain untamable wilderness.

With all the modern technology at our fingertips in the twenty-first century, satellites, GPS, radios, radar, emergency beacons, Coast Guard helicopters, and survival suits, men still set sail in this region with a sense of foreboding.

Only 2 percent of the ocean floor has been explored. To date, twelve men have walked on the moon which is two hundred thousand miles from Earth; yet as of 2010, only two men have ever traveled to the deepest point of the ocean (35,840 feet), and neither of them ever set foot there. On January 23, 1960, U.S. Navy Lt. Don Walsh and Jacques Piccard on board the USS *Trieste*, a bathyscaphe submersible, reached the bottom of the Marianas Trench, the deepest known point of any ocean in the world, after a four-hour descent.

Halfway down, the outer pane of the double-glass viewing port of the sub cracked from the pressure, leaving only one pane of glass between them and instant death; even if that one would fail, they incredibly decided to continue to the bottom. At the bottom, the pressure on the hull was eight tons per square inch. They were shocked to see flounder, sole, and shrimp at these incredible depths and pressures. That was the only manned decent to the deepest point of the ocean in the history of mankind.

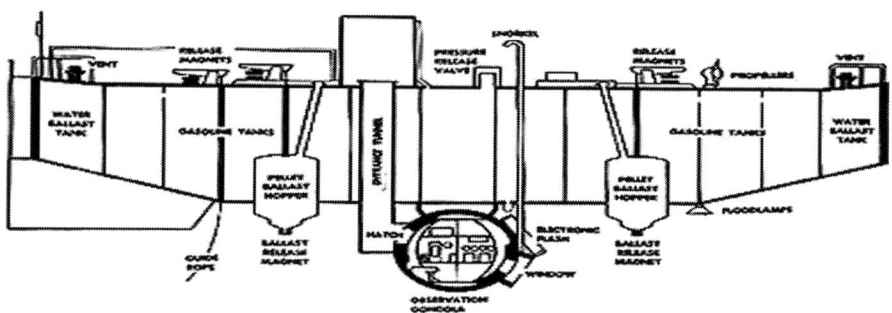

USS *Trieste*

The ocean contains the greatest mountain ranges and volcanoes on Earth, stretching for thousands of miles and are a half-mile higher than Mount Everest which is twenty-nine thousand feet high. Yet these are swallowed up like a pebble thrown into a pond.

Sailors often whisper of mysterious rogue waves that can sink the largest ships all by themselves. Marine scientists have largely dismissed this talk as superstition or fantasy despite the fact that over the last twenty years, more than two hundred supercarriers and cargo ships over six hundred feet long have been lost at sea, many without a trace. Those with eyewitness reports suggest many were sunk by huge, violent walls of water that rose up out of a calm sea.

On average, two large ships are sunk every week, according to the GKSS Research Centre in Geestacht, Germany. Incredibly the causes are never studied in detail the same as air crashes. They simply are logged as being due to "bad weather."

To prove the phenomenon or lay the rumors to rest, a group of eleven organizations from six European Union countries founded MaxWave in December 2000. As part of the project, two Earth-scanning satellites, ERS 1 and ERS 2, were used to monitor the oceans with their radar. During a three-week period in 2001, around thirty thousand images were taken and analyzed. The survey revealed ten massive waves one hundred feet high.

The evidence stunned the scientific community. Their conclusion was these waves exist in much higher numbers than anyone expected. The fact that rogue waves actually occur relatively frequently has had major safety and economic implications around the world. It took satellites to confirm what sailors had always instinctively known; no ship is safe from the ocean's raw power. Arriving safely at port is only at the mercy of the sea.

All of us have heard at one time or another that the Earth is a water planet. Yet experiencing the shift in our consciousness from a land-based to an ocean-based one is experienced by few. Today hundreds of thousands of people cross the world's oceans in hours instead of weeks or months, in total comfort, never having to brace themselves from incoming waves or feel the spray of saltwater in their face. The ocean has become a distant flat blue plain, to be glanced at occasionally from a plane window at thirty thousand feet while sipping a drink and watching a movie.

As a child growing up in the deserts of Arizona, I had a fascination for and love of ships, especially sailing ships of the eighteenth century. I remember having books with beautiful paintings of clipper ships under full sail majestically riding the crest of white-foamed waves as they raced across the Pacific to China.

One of my first memories as a child of seeing real ships was when I was five; my parents had taken a vacation at Mission Beach in

San Diego, California. The day we left to return to Phoenix was a dark, overcast morning with thick fog along the coast. As we drove away from the beach, I was in the backseat looking out the back window. We were on a hill, and I had a panoramic view out to sea and could just make out on the horizon the dark grey silhouettes of navy warships against the lighter grey fog. A feeling of mystery and adventure swept over me, and a longing to be on one of those ships was overwhelming.

When I was eighteen, two of my best friends and I drove a pickup truck to Alaska. In those days, the Alcan Highway that starts in British Columbia, Canada, wasn't paved yet. We drove fifteen hundred miles on a dirt and mud road to the Alaskan border. One of my friend's older brothers lived in Anchorage, and he had asked me if I'd like to drive up that summer (1974) with him for a visit. I jumped at the offer, and we arrived that June. We ended up camping out in a park in downtown Anchorage on the shore of Cook Inlet.

A tent city had sprung up with hundreds of people from all over the country looking for work on the Trans-Alaska Pipeline that was beginning to be built that summer. One day my friends returned to camp to inform me that they had just been hired to go to the Arctic and work on the pipeline. If I hurried down to the office, I could get a job as well. I had other plans, much to their dismay.

The week prior to that, I had been visiting the local Coast Guard recruiter downtown and had made up my mind that my time had come to go to sea. A week later, we said our good-byes as they were about to board a plane to Dead Horse on the Arctic coast of Alaska, and I was flying to San Francisco for Coast Guard boot camp.

My shift from a land-based consciousness to an ocean one came unexpectedly as a seaman aboard the Coast Guard Cutter *Northwind*, an icebreaker 282-feet long with wooden decks. The *Northwind* was a relic of a bygone era when I arrived aboard her in 1975. She was the last of the Wind-class icebreakers; the *Eastwind, Southwind*, and *Westwind* icebreakers had already been scrapped. All had been built in the 1920s, and the first of a new class of icebreaker was already commissioned, the modern Polar Class.

I was a young seaman aboard the *Northwind* as we sailed from Baltimore, Maryland, on a six-month Arctic patrol off the coast of Greenland and a mission to break ice on the St. Lawrence River to the Great Lakes. It was on that voyage, my first on the deep ocean, that I came to realize that for all the land the Earth has, it truly is an ocean planet. Week after week of traveling hundreds of miles and seeing only water as far as the eye could see in every direction and knowing that there was incredible depth to that water was like contemplating the stars in the sky.

We made port at St. John's, Newfoundland, after a week of smooth sailing north from Maryland. After several days there, we cast off and began to make our way out from the protection of the harbor to the open ocean. Shortly after leaving the pier, the captain came over the PA system and gave us orders to batten down all loose equipment and all hatches as we were going to be sailing into a storm as we reached the ocean.

Being eighteen and from Arizona, I had no idea what was about to transpire. So as I made my way out onto the deck to lash down gear, I wasn't prepared for what I saw as I opened the hatch and stepped out. We weren't even completely out of the harbor yet, but the scene before me took my breath away, and I was momentarily frozen in awe. Beautiful beyond description, the swells we were sailing over were mountainous; for the first time, the ship that was my world and my security became very tiny and very fragile.

We rose up upon one of the giant waves I could see for miles out to the distant horizon then the ship would roll down the side of the wave as we dipped down into the deep valley between swells. All I could see then were thirty-five-foot walls of water towering all around me until I was sure we'd be swallowed up. At the last seemingly possible moment before I was sure we'd all be sent to the bottom to the ocean, the ship would begin to rise up the side of the next mountain of water, and the whole process would repeat itself. The raw, overwhelming power of nature was unbelievable.

We finally made our way out from the protection of the harbor. The ferocity of the storm began to increase rapidly and to a level that left me cowering inside the galley, peering out a porthole with increasing fear for my life. I can never forget having to look up from the porthole to find the top of the waves which were thirty-five feet high. Hurricane-force winds tore the tops off the towering walls of water like shotgun blast.

For several days, life became so miserable and full of the fear; death seemed a welcome way out of the hell the ocean was putting us through. We had to crawl on the decks to get anywhere. You simply could not stand or walk more than a few feet at a time and only if you hung on to an immovable object with all your strength. We could not eat or sleep, and we were all absolutely exhausted. The toilets were backed up and overflowing in the heads, and the filth sloshed back and forth across the decks.

Several men were injured being thrown against machinery, breaking bones and having internal injuries. They were flown to hospitals by the two helicopters we carried on board. Most of the crew were seasick, I included, and I was violently seasick to the point that I was so weak I could not stand and so miserable I didn't care if I lived or died. For several days, I tied myself into my bunk and held on for dear life.

It was there in the midst of the tempest that I thought back to the men who sailed the wooden sailing ships of centuries past, realizing for the first time what incredible people they were. One night a friend who was a radio operator and had a bunk under mine told me that a gauge on the bridge measuring the angle of list the ship takes was registering fifty degrees; our ship would capsize at fifty-two degrees. It was a long, terrifying night.

I couldn't believe that in the modern age, with all our advanced technology, the ocean still had complete power over those who dared set sail upon her waters. I had no idea what people had to go through to travel on the ocean until then, and I was amazed people would choose to do so after what I had learned those past few days. A deep appreciation for those men's courage and sense of dedication grew as my ordeal unfolded. Those were truly the days of wooden ships and steel men.

The next month we spent crashing thru the frozen Arctic Sea off the coast of Greenland. When we finally returned to Baltimore, this boy from the deserts of Arizona had come to realize this was truly an ocean planet.

There never was a great man yet
who spent all his life on land.

—Herman Melville

Chapter 3

Naming the Void

St. Peter

Adecade and a half later, as a maritime medic sailing on the Bering Sea, I could hardly imagine what it must have been like for Captain-Commander Vitus Bering to set sail onto what was then a black void. The expedition of Vitus Bering is one of the least taught stories yet one of the most courageous and unbelievable journeys in history. When he and his men set sail from Siberia, they might as well have been traveling to Mars or beyond.

The maps that Bering had to rely on were hopelessly unreliable, inaccurate, and vague. No one knew the size of the American continent nor the North Pacific Ocean nor the unnamed body of water in between.

It was Peter the Great of Russia who wanted to know what lay beyond the void; perhaps he could expand his empire, or who knew what riches might be gained?

Vitus Bering was Danish. To support his family, he had joined the new Russian Navy in his early twenties. He had over the years proved to be a capable seaman who rose in rank to a lieutenant. He eventually drew the attention of Peter the Great and was chosen to lead an expedition to see if the Russian and American continents were joined at some point, as rumors vaguely suggested.

In 1728, Bering set off on his first expedition north from Kamchatka through the straits that now bear his name up to Siberia's East Cape. Vitus Bering's main concerns were the safety of his crew and the safe return of his ship. Bering was above all a sailor and concerned with the lives of his men. This is by no means to suggest that Vitus Bering was not an extremely brave man with tremendous will. Just to get to the Sea of Okhotsk, Bering led eighty men across five thousand miles of Siberian wilderness.

When they reached the western shore of the Sea of Okhotsk, they built a small ship, the *Fortuna*, and they sailed across to Kamchatka. Unsure of the way south around the Kamchatka Peninsula, they incredibly dismantled the *Fortuna* and carried its hardware and rigging over the mountains to the eastern coast of Kamchatka. This journey alone was absolutely incredible in its own right and took years to accomplish under the most difficult of conditions. Yet Bering was not finished; his crew built another very small vessel, the *Sviatoi Gavriil* (St. Gabriel), from the parts of the *Fortuna* they had carried over the mountain ranges of Kamchatka.

In his book, *Alaska: An American Colony*, Stephen Haycox wrote that the *Sviatoi Gavriil* was not an ocean-capable vessel because Bering believed that if the Siberian land mass was connected to another, it would be north of them; and he would sail along the coast to find it. As he sailed farther north, he feared he would be trapped in the ice of the coming winter and decided to turn back.

Upon his return, he was scorned as having achieved little for the expense and time invested and was publically discredited. That could have been the end of Bering's story except as fate would have it, he requested another chance to redeem himself. Empress Anna who succeeded Peter the Great did just that, and in 1731, he was given command of a second expedition.

Ironically this was when Bering's troubles really began; he might have fared better fading from the pages of history and growing old in the comfort of home and what was left of his family as historical accounts confirm Bering's five sons died during this period.

The incredible situation with Captain Bering was his voyage had to begin with another five-thousand-mile, cross-country journey across the world's most remote and desolate wilderness before he even set eyes on any ocean. This journey from St. Petersburg to Kamchatka took three years and crossed vast expanses of swamp and tundra windswept with subzero winds and blowing drifts of deep snow. By the time he reached Avacha Bay on the Kamchatka Peninsula, his spirit was broken, and he was racked with numerous illnesses including a deep depression.

In May 1741, the *St. Peter* and the *St. Paul*, both almost identical at being eighty feet long, set sail. Each carried a crew of seventy-seven and seventy-six men respectively. After almost two weeks at sea, they had developed a fierce allegiance to each other until one day, as the

St. Paul passed ahead of the *St. Peter* in a dense fog, the two ships lost sight of each other; and neither one ever saw the other again.

The captains of both ships gave orders for their vessels to search for the other but to no avail. The captain of the *St. Paul* was Alexei Chirikov, the same man who had been Bering's second-in-command on Bering's failed first expedition. He made a half-hearted effort to look for the *St. Peter* and after two days gave the order to continue east. He had lost confidence in Bering's cautious ways and was determined not to fail this time. To him, Bering was a Dane; and Chirikov, being Russian, felt the fame of any discovery should go to a Russian. Finally free of Bering's shadow, he set sail to find the American continent.

Bering, on the other hand, was deeply disturbed by the loss of their sister ship. He felt it imperative that both ships should remain together in those unknown waters. On the third day of searching, Bering decided to continue with their original mission and set course to the east.

St. Peter and St. Paul, Bering Sea, 1741

Both ships eventually sighted land which turned out to be Alaska. About this time, both ships were dangerously low on fresh water; on sighting land, procuring fresh supplies of drinking water would take priority before any exploration was to take place.

On July 16, the *St. Paul* was off the coast of Alaska. On the 18th, they sighted land, and it was decided to put a boat ashore. In the following attempts to put a group of men on the beach, Captain Chirikov lost one-third of his crew and both of his small boats after the first one and then another boat disappeared as they entered a bay in an attempt to land on the beach.

After these disasters, Chirikov had no choice except to immediately set sail back to Kamchatka. With both small boats gone, they had no way to put anyone onshore. Although the *St. Paul* could get to within a quarter-mile of land in places, and Chirikov and his men could see and smell the green trees and rivers of fresh water emptying in the sea, they might as well have been a million miles away. So began a race against time and death to get back to Avacha Bay in Kamchatka. On the desperate voyage back, half the remaining crew died of scurvy and malnutrition when the *St. Paul* finally sailed into Avacha Bay. The ship was in tatters, and the survivors barely alive.

Chirikov barely survived the voyage and remained on the Kamchatka Peninsula too sick to return to St. Petersburg and died several years later, any fame of discovery dying with him. Captain Bering on board the *St. Peter* sailed onward. The morning was foggy, and visibility was only a few hundred feet. Finally the fog lifted and revealed the *St. Peter* to be only a few miles off the coast of land consisting of the majestic snow-covered peaks of Alaska.

The joy of the crew of the *St. Peter* was overwhelming as we might imagine, yet Captain Bering stood motionless on deck expressionless, gazing at the continent he had spent the past ten years of his life to find. Already racked with depression and countless ailments and totally exhausted, Bering probably realized at that moment that he had no more to give. With his men gathered around congratulating him, he turned and staggered back to his cabin.

It took several days waiting out bad weather and searching for the best place to put a small boat ashore to finally get a shore party to the beach. The men's mission was to get fresh water and return to the *St. Peter* as soon as possible. It had taken them almost two months to reach America, and the expedition was behind schedule. They had lost the *St. Paul*, and they were scheduled to return to Kamchatka by September. It logically would take them as long to return, if not longer; they had about three weeks left if they were to stay on schedule. To map the coastline of America was already an impossible task.

Bering had all this on his mind as his men were ashore. One of the men onshore was the famous naturalist, Georg Steller, who had dreamed of that moment most of his life. Being the first to document the unique wildlife of America, Steller was having the time of his life. After only ten hours, all the men onshore were ordered to return to the *St. Peter* anchored nearby. Steller was furious and lingered as long as he could in an attempt to gather as many specimens as possible. Threatened with being left behind unless he returned immediately, he finally boarded the small boat and returned to the *St. Peter*.

Bering was responsible for the safety of his crew and had no interest in Steller's mission. They were there to map and survey the coast for future expeditions and lay claim for the Russian Empire. Captain Bering, as stated earlier, was a brave man, that was clear from his achievements getting to Alaska, yet he did not have the nautical experience as some of the other well-known explorers like Captain Cook or Captain Vancouver. He didn't have the confidence, probably rightly so, to linger any longer so far from home. After taking everything into consideration, he decided that night to return to Kamchatka. The next morning, he gave the order to pull up the anchor and set sail west, much to the dismay of Steller but no doubt to the relief of most of his crew.

After sacrificing ten years of his life and enduring unimaginable hardships and without setting foot on the new continent, Bering's moment in history had come and gone. Lethargic and with sunken, grey, hollow eyes, he returned to his bunk and fell asleep.

From that day on, Bering would spend the entire voyage in his cabin, having given full responsibility over to his second-in-command. They already were in complete survival mode. Low on drinking water and being in completely uncharted waters, they blindly made their way the best they could in a westerly direction. They were at the mercy of the changing, unfavorable winds; and they sailed erratically, first west then south, dodging the many islands that blocked their way home.

Soon scurvy broke out, and the crew grew more and more lethargic and inefficient in their task. Their ship was battered by increasing gales and severe squalls. They were forced to change course or drift; they made almost no progress. They were forced to land again on what is now one of the Shumigan Islands off the Alaskan Peninsula, in another rushed attempt to fill their water casks. They filled them with the first water they found on the island, which turned out to be brackish and contaminated with saltwater from the nearby ocean.

Losing more precious time, they were increasingly battling gale-force headwinds; many of the crew were in the advanced stages of scurvy and malnutrition. As the weather grew worse, the ship was overwhelmed by increasingly fierce gales, and the small ship was battered by howling winds which shredded sail and rigging. The suffering of the crew was by then unimaginable; unable to eat or sleep from being tossed mercilessly by the increasingly savage seas, the crew grew weaker and weaker.

It was already mid-October, and the winds had turned bitter cold with flurries of snow. The crew was so weak that maintaining control of the ship was becoming impossible, including the necessary chart navigation.

The westernmost islands of the Aleutians were spotted on October 13. By now they had lost track of exactly where they were and mistook these to be the Kuril Islands that lay just south of Kamchatka. Actually if they had continued west, they would have reached Avacha Bay in a week's time. Instead they turned north, thinking they were sailing toward the Kamchatka Peninsula. A few days later, they spotted land again, concluding this was finally Kamchatka. As the skies cleared that afternoon, they were able to take an observation of their position from the sun. Only then did they realize that they were still several hundred miles east of their destination.

St. Peter, Bering Sea, 1741

If anyone was to survive, it was decided to attempt to land on these islands as soon as possible. With the entire crew so weak as to barely stand, the *St. Peter* was allowed to just drift toward the island. Soon a sound like thunder was heard from the massive waves crashing on the jagged shoreline. Cries went up from men who realized they were about to die, and their cries mixed with the sound of howling winds and thunderous seas. At the last moment, before the ship was to be dashed against the rocks, something amazing happened, perhaps a small miracle. A huge wave lifted the ship up and over the rock-strewn reef, and the ship settled onto a sand-bottomed placid tidal lake; the *St. Peter*, finally grounded safely on the island, would never sail again.

The next day, those that could began to make their way to dry land. So sick were most of the crew that as many left the ship's putrid holds and reached the beach, they collapsed and died on the spot as they breathed the fresh frigid air. It took over a week to get all the crew to shore where they discovered shallow caves dug into sand dunes by fox that inhabited the island. These they would dig out, making them able to seek shelter, and would be their homes throughout the long winter.

On December 8, Captain Vitus Bering finally succumbed to his long battle with his many illnesses, including by then severe scurvy and malnutrition. He had refused to eat any of the green plants that Steller had offered him. Steller knew they were high in vitamin C and could cure Bering and had tried to convince his captain of their benefits, to no avail. He was thousands of miles from his home and hadn't seen his family in ten long, grueling years; now the snow-covered mountains of this lonely island were to be his gravestone.

After several scouting trips around the island, they found there was plenty of driftwood and wildlife on the island for food—seals, sea lions, otters, birds, and thousands of blue fox. As winter set in, the beaches were covered with several feet of snow, and howling winds made starting fires almost impossible. Against all odds, they managed to hold on.

What ended up saving the crew was the presence of Georg Steller. A naturalist, he alone knew of the medicinal qualities of the indigenous plants on the island. He finally convinced the crew, largely out of their own hunger, to begin eating what he had been offering such as cranberry and wintergreen leaves dug from the snow and made into a tea. He also provided fresh roots and bulbs in their diets and insisted they drink only fresh clean water. As their strength returned, they were able to hunt sea lions and seals.

In January 1742, the scurvy plague claimed one last victim, reaching a total of thirty-one dead out of a crew of seventy-seven men. Then plans were debated on how they might be able to return to Kamchatka.

Finally they came up with the idea to use the lumber from the already grounded *St. Peter* to build a smaller boat. Winter slowly gave way to spring, and the incredible work began in earnest to build a new boat. Providence was with them again as the only ship right on the crew had survived, making it possible for the survivors to build a boat from the wreck of the *St. Peter*. The new ship, actually a boat, was only forty-one feet long from stem to stern and eleven feet wide at the beam.

On August 8, 1742, the men were able to get the boat into the water and set sail for Kamchatka. Fourteen days after leaving "Bering" island and bailing constantly to keep the leaky vessel afloat, forty-one of the original seventy-seven men dropped anchor in the inner harbor of Avacha Bay, Kamchatka, bringing the expedition and one of the most incredible stories of survival to an end.

Eventually in the pages of history, the once unknown void that appeared blank on the world's maps became known as the Bering Sea. Just since the 1970s, over 2,500 vessels of all sizes rest on her bottom, scattered with the bones of hundreds of men. Today as in 1741, there is still a moment of pause before the lines from the pier are cast off.

The ocean is a hard teacher. She gives the
test first, then the lesson.

Chapter 4

The Beginning

Seattle

Paramedics and E.M.T.s wanted to work on ships sailing to the Soviet Far East. Bering Sea and Sea of Okhotsk, knowledge of emergency medicine with at least one year experience required. 60 to 90 day contracts, extremely remote, working long hours, excellent pay. (*Seattle Times*, August 9, 1991)

This ad really caught my eye. It was hardly the kind of want ad seen in the paper. Even in a major port city like Seattle, this was a rare find and one I wasn't going to let pass me by if I could help it.

"Why are you looking at the want ads?" my partner asked as he sat next to me in the cab of our ambulance. We were in downtown Seattle waiting for our next call on a quiet Sunday morning. "Don't you like this job?" he asked.

"Sure, I like this job," I replied. "I always look in the want ads. It's an old habit of mine." I continued, "You never know what else might be out there that could better your life."

Anxious but doing my best to remain calm, I looked back to the open paper with excitement. Quickly scanning the small print, I found the ad again amid the dozens of others. Medics needed to sail to Kamchatka, without ever knowing how it would present itself, without knowing the details. I knew this was what I always wanted to do; I knew then my time had come.

The next day, Monday, August 10, I called the number in the ad and made an appointment to be seen for an interview later that afternoon. There I met Susan, the personal representative of Arctic Ice Fisheries.

I had a good interview. I was more than qualified. I had three years as an EMT III answering 911 calls in the greater Seattle area. I had state certifications in IV, ACLS (Advanced Cardiac Life Support) and Swift Water Rescue. I had emergency medical experience from responding to hundreds of 911 calls and was hired on the spot.

During the interview, it was explained to me that the Soviet fishing grounds in the Far East were being opened to U.S. fishing fleets. For the then-faltering Soviet economy to increase their revenue, the Russian government had made the desperate decision to allow foreign vessels into what was up until then completely restricted areas. These waters had been closed for seventy years as long as the Soviet communists had been in power. They had many highly sensitive military bases scattered over the Kamchatka Peninsula and Siberian mainland.

In 1983, a Korean airliner, a 747 with 269 people on board that was unknowingly flying off course over the restricted Kamchatka Peninsula and the Sea of Okhotsk, was shot down by Russian fighter jets, killing everyone on board. This would be the very area that we'd be fishing in the near future.

Arctic Ice Fisheries had purchased a two-million-pound king crab quota from the Russian government and was sending the 110-foot crab catcher/processor *Royal Enterprise* to the Sea of Okhotsk, USSR, to catch the quota. It would have a crew of twenty-four having the ability to catch crab as well as process the live crab using brine cookers, cooking and then packaging the crab legs into ninety-five-pound cases, freezing and then storing the crab in a freezer hold. When the freezer hold was full, the *Royal Enterprise* would then travel the short distance to the Kuril Islands south of the Sea of Okhotsk and off-load the product onto cargo ships. This would enable the *Royal Enterprise* to stay in the area and quickly catch the quota and then return to Seattle.

Although we would have access to the fishing grounds offshore, we would not be allowed onshore at any time. In case of any emergency other than sinking, we'd be on our own. It would take the *Royal Enterprise* seven days to reach Dutch Harbor in the Aleutian Islands in Alaska, and then it was another eight-hundred-mile flight to Anchorage to the nearest hospital.

To help ensure that the *Royal Enterprise* could stay on station fishing, in case of an illness or injury to a crew member, it was decided to have a trauma—and illness-trained medical person on board the trip. That was where I would come in.

The next morning, I came back to the office to read and sign my contract and fill out my W-4. I signed a ninety-day contract where I would be paid $200 a day to perform medical duties only. I'd be on call 24/7. As I reached the exit as I was leaving, the secretary behind the counter called out to me, "Hey, would you be interested in making a lot more money?"

I stopped halfway out the door and slowly stepped back into the lobby. "More money?" I said and walked back over to her desk. "How?"

"The *Royal Enterprise* is short a crewman. One of the regular guys can't make this trip. If you sign on as a crewman, you would receive a percentage of the catch. On a quota of two million pounds, that's a lot of money. Interested?"

"I've never worked on a crab boat before," I responded, thinking that would put the issue to rest right there.

"Do you have any experience working on boats?" she asked.

"Well, yes, I spent some time on an icebreaker in the Coast Guard."

"That's good enough. You'll be shown what to do when the time comes," she responded and continued. "It can really boring out there just sitting around. Working on deck will make the time fly by a lot faster."

I didn't realize how the next several seconds would affect my life as I quickly pondered the offer. All I was thinking about was the money. If I had known what I was getting into, I would surely have refused. As fate would have it, I didn't have a clue then.

"Where do I sign?" I asked.

"Right here, on this line," she replied. "Sign right here."

No matter how important a man at sea may consider himself, unless he is fundamentally worthy, the sea will someday find him out.

—Felix Riesenberg

Chapter 5

M/V Royal Enterprise

A week later, at the end of August, I arrived at the pier where the *Royal Enterprise* was docked. It was a typical drizzly, overcast morning. There was a lot of activity around and on board the ship as I carried my gear up the gangway.

Forklifts on the docks scurried back and forth, and cranes lifted pallets of supplies from the pier onto the deck of the boat. Flashes from welding torches at various places on the vessel forced me to keep turning my head to avoid eye contact with the welder's flame. Pneumatic air hoses, welding hoses, various pieces of equipment and compressors, tools, and scrap metal made it difficult to make my way across the deck and stay out of the way of all the activity taking place around me.

I figured the wheelhouse would be the best place to check in, but I wasn't sure of the best way to get there. I caught the eye of a passing guy who appeared he might be a member of the crew. "Hey, how do I get to the wheelhouse?" I quickly asked before he had a chance to get away.

He started to give me directions then seeing the look on my face, he stopped in midsentence realizing the folly in explaining the complicated layout of the ship to a greenhorn like myself. Somewhat annoyed, he said, "Follow me, I'll take you there." I followed him through the narrow passageway up a flight of metal steps to the wheelhouse. Before I could thank the guy for bringing me up there, he turned and vanished out the way we had come.

There I met Mike, the deck boss. He was a big man, around six foot four or so and around 250 pounds. He had a large barrel chest, a large black beard, and black shaggy hair sticking out from under a worn-out, dirty ball cap. The skin of his face was etched with lines and wrinkles, resembling worn leather from his years at sea exposed to the wind and saltwater.

He walked over to where I was, and we shook hands, holding our grip for a moment while we sized each other up. "My name's Mike," he finally said.

"Hey, good to meet you. My name is Erick. I'll be your medic on this voyage."

"Well, I guess the first thing to do is get your gear stowed and find a bunk," he said. "Then you'll need to get an inventory of the medical supplies we have on board and make a list of what you think you're going to need. Give it to me as soon as possible, so we can get it on board. We're scheduled to leave in two days, so you'd better get right on it." With that I started to get organized and prepared for our departure.

I had never prepared a ship for its medical needs before, and they had never had a medic on any of their previous voyages, so I was making an educated guess on what it was I would need and how much. If I missed something and it turned out we did need it, and things turned bad, it would be my fault. I began to feel the pressure I would be under most of the trip, being responsible for the welfare of the crew and keeping the ship from having to abort its voyage and return to Dutch Harbor if someone really got hurt bad.

Also, these guys had been fishing for years without a trained medic on board and were skeptical of the need for me. The captain didn't feel we needed anything more than the basic first aid kit they had always carried on board, so getting anything was going to be a challenge. After some convincing, I was able to get him to agree on suture kits, antibiotics, and pain meds. I had to remind him that where we were going, there was not going to be any U.S. Coast Guard coming to our rescue as he had been used to in the Alaskan Sea. What finally did the trick was reminding him of the money we could lose if we had to return to Dutch if I was unable to successfully treat a serious injury.

This had seemed obvious to me, and I was surprised that I had to convince the captain. I sensed that these men took pride in their toughness and ability to endure hardship and pain and didn't take kindly to any suggestion that they might need someone like me to look after them. I realized that I was going to have to prove myself to these men and hoped I'd be up to the challenge.

In the week before I arrived on board, I had a five-day training period at Swedish Hospital in Seattle with Dr. Martin, an emergency room physician and the owner of a private company, Maritime Health Services. I not only was given some training on some of the possible emergency procedures I might have to administer at sea that I was not trained in, such as suturing. I was also briefed on some of the possible medical supplies I might need as well.

Maritime Health Services is a company that helps facilitates any aspect of medical care that might be needed by a vessel at sea, such as information on what to do for any given emergency procedure and arranging for transportation to the proper medical facility if a crewman needed to be evacuated from the ship or any advice. I would be in contact with Dr. Martin on a fairly regular basis throughout the trip. I made a call to him to get his advice on a list of items I'd need and then ordered them.

Trawler leaving Seattle

As the day arrived for us to leave, I awoke pretty excited. It turned out to be a beautiful day. Around nine thirty that morning, we were ready to go. I joined the crew on deck to help cast off the lines that held us to the pier. One at a time, they were hauled in; and the *Royal Enterprise*, 110-feet long, slowly moved away from the dock and got underway.

As we moved out into Elliot Bay, we had a panoramic view of downtown Seattle, called the Emerald City and with a beautiful skyline. Soon it was passing behind us as we made our way into Puget Sound. A strong feeling of adventure swelled in my chest as we stowed the mooring lines below and prepared the ship for the open ocean.

By that afternoon, we were nearing the Pacific Ocean as we passed the high snow-capped mountains of the Olympic Mountain range on the Washington State coast. As the sun was setting over the western horizon, the *Royal Enterprise*'s bow began to slice through the white-capped waves of the Pacific. The wind carried the salt spray of the waves over the bow, drenching the forward decks and the wheelhouse with ice-cold water. We were on a north by northeast heading bound for our first destination, Dutch Harbor, Alaska.

It was a seven-day voyage to Dutch Harbor. The weather remained good the entire way. Clear skies and sunshine greeted us each morning as we continued north. The crew settled into a routine on twelve-hour shifts. Our main entertainment at night was watching movies in the galley on VHS tapes on the ship's VCR. Most of our time was spent working in the processing area where the equipment used to cook and freeze the crab had to be cleaned, reassembled, and made ready for the coming season.

Each night I'd make it a point to step out on deck and get some fresh air and a little quiet time. That shift to an ocean consciousness slowly began to take hold as I gazed at the seemingly endless plain of water day after day, night after night. I'd felt it before many years earlier as a young seaman; then it was returning with a feeling of how immense the oceans were and how small and very far away I was.

We pulled into Unalaska Bay on the morning of September 2 around seven thirty in the morning and tied up at the pier. Dutch Harbor is located on Amaknak Island. There are no trees that grow naturally on the Aleutians. The rolling hills and 5,500-foot volcano are covered with a tall, thick carpet of beautiful green grass sprinkled with a variety of wildflowers and wild berries. These islands are almost continually covered in fog and mist, and it rains around 250 inches a year, making it one of the wettest places in the United States. As luck would have it, that day was a rare sunny, beautiful day.

We'd spend several days there loading our crab pots and food, salt and "fiber," the cardboard boxes that the crab legs would be packed in.

Our shifts were changed there to sixteen hours a day staggered as we needed to onload and set sail as soon as possible. This schedule would mean loading operations could continue twenty-four hours a day until the job was finished. The crew split into sections that started eight hours apart, ensured we'd have the manpower to accomplish this. No time is wasted on fishing boats; as soon as we were tied to the docks, trucks started to arrive with the tons of supplies we'd need on our three-month voyage. If I hadn't signed on as a crewman, I could be in the galley watching movies as the loading operations were underway, making $200 dollars a day. It then dawned on me the consequences of my decision in Seattle.

I was in pretty good shape. I was thirty-four years old, six foot tall and weighed around 175 pounds. I wasn't a stranger to hard work and had done plenty of it in my time, although it had been a few years already since I had really done any. All that was about to change as from thereon out. I'd be introduced to a level and intensity of work few people in this modern age ever experience. It would test me to my limits and beyond.

There is nothing more dangerous
than a resourceful idiot

—Scott Raymond Adams

Chapter 6

A fist full of Dynamite

Dutch Harbor, Alaska

As it turned out, I wouldn't start my sixteen-hour shift for another eight hours. I made my way to the galley before retiring to my bunk. There I ran into the deck boss, Mike, and the first engineer, Chris. They were talking about going for drive with the company pickup truck and finding a spot to do some target shooting. I quickly realized that this might be my last chance to get off the boat for months before we set sail again. I knew I'd need all the rest I could get before my shift started, but I really wanted to explore the island. The way I saw it, I'd never have the chance again, so I asked if I could go along.

"Yeah, sure, Doc. Let's get going, so we can get back in time to get some sleep."

As we made our way down the gangway to the dock, several semitrucks with trailers were already on the pier maneuvering into position to off-load their contents onto the *Royal Enterprise*. The ship's crane was being swung out to get into position, and several forklifts were moving about positioning themselves as well. As we darted in between all this activity careful not to get ourselves run over, I pushed the eventual reality of the work that lay ahead to the back of my mind.

I was too excited right then at the chance to explore one of the Aleutian Islands. I imagined that this was how Georg Steller must have felt when he had the chance to get off the *St. Peter* and explore this same region in 1741. The target practice was going to be fun. I enjoyed shooting, but I was far more filled with the mind-set of adventure and seeing new and exotic places.

We climbed into the cab of the truck and made our way onto the dirt road heading away from town. The road was right along the coast of the island; on one side was Unalaska Bay and on the other the immediate slopes and cliffs of the island's mountains. We twisted and turned on the bumpy road for about twenty minutes until we spotted an area to pull off the road on the island side.

The area was a clearing partially carved out of the hillside, about sixty feet in diameter. In the far turn in the arc was what appeared to be a bunker cut into the side of the hill. At the beginning of World War II, Dutch Harbor was a busy naval and air base which was bombed by the Japanese in June 1941. The island had scores of concrete pillboxes and gun emplacements along with different kinds of old military bunkers scattered around the island.

This looked like one of those bunkers. Seeing how we had come to do some shooting for the moment, we ignored the bunker and prepared to start some target practice. Chris and Mike had brought along a Smith and Wesson .44 caliber revolver, a .30.06 M1 carbine, and a pump-action 12-gauge shotgun. As luck would have it, the turnout was scattered with aluminum cans and pieces of scrap lumber. Seeing all the bullet holes in these, it was clear we were not the first to have the same idea.

We set up our targets and for the next half hour blazed away. After a while, our attention was drawn to the bunker door, and curiosity pulled us the entrance of the bunker. That's when we noticed much to our surprise that the padlock on the door was broken and hung unlocked on the latch. Naturally we slowly pushed open the creaking heavy door as the sunlight from outside illuminated the inside of the bunker. The air from inside was dank, humid, and had the heavy smell of decay.

The bunker, far from being empty as we had first thought, was filled with wooden crates stacked neatly on both sides of the bunker with a space to walk in between. Several had the wooded slats on their tops pulled off and scattered around on the ground. Red warning labels on some of the crates read "Explosives." We walked over and looked into one of the open boxes. Inside were nine-inch-long, half-inch-diameter brown sticks of what appeared to be dynamite stacked neatly. Mike reached in and picked one out. Upon closer inspection, we could see beads of sweat covering the stick and all the rest in the case as well.

As Mike and Chris took turns handling the stick, I began to realize that the beads of liquid were nitroglycerine leaching out of old and very unstable sticks of dynamite. I'm not exactly sure where I had learned that; probably from one of the History Channel shows called *Modern Marvels*, about the history of explosives that I'd seen recently back home in Seattle. However I knew it, I was convinced this was not a good thing. I was sure it would be obvious to the others as well as I expressed my concern that we shouldn't be handling them and should leave right away.

Instead, as I was turning to leave, I heard Mike say, "Hey, let's take a case or two back to the boat."

"Yeah," Chris eagerly agreed.

Mike continued to explain his brilliant plan. "After we leave Dutch Harbor, we can throw a case overboard and watch it explode in the ocean behind us."

Chris added, "Yeah, we can strap the case to a pallet and drop it over the side with the pot launcher. It will explode off the stern."

"That's a great idea," Mike said as he bent over and picked up a case.

"Hey, look over here. These are detonators and fuses," Chris pointed out as he eagerly continued to look around the stacks of boxes.

"Cool! Grab some. We'll need them to set this baby off."

"What the hell are you guys talking about?" I chimed in. "This stuff is really unstable. Do you want to get us all killed?" There was a moment of silence as they both stopped what they were doing and turned to face me.

"Are you some kind of pussy?" Chris finally said.

"Yeah, Doc. What's your problem?" Mike added.

"My problem is I don't want to die," I replied.

"Well, this isn't your call, Doc, so relax," was Mike's reply as they continued to gather up everything they were going to take with them. As they finished deciding all they were going to take, I left the bunker and went out to wait by the truck. It might offer some protection from a blast if they blew themselves up inside the bunker.

After a few minutes, they came out carrying two boxes, both filled with fifty sticks of dynamite sweating nitro and some blasting caps and fuses. As they came over to the truck, I suggested they make a cushion for the cases in the bed of the truck with some of the fishing nets and buoys that were back there. It would cushion the dynamite from some of the vibration and bumps from the potholes in the road on our way back. To my relief, they agreed to that.

"This is crazy," I muttered to myself as we climbed into the cab of the truck. Mike immediately put the truck into gear, and we backed out onto the dirt road, bouncing in and out of a large pothole in the process. My heart jumped into my throat as I braced myself for the explosion I was sure would follow.

Mike then threw the truck into forward, and we sped off down the road, a tan trail of fine dust blowing behind us. Chris lit up a cigarette while Mike began to tell us about his last drunk at a bar in Dutch Harbor last time he was there.

In the meantime, I sat between the two of them focused on the road, mentally driving the truck, trying to avoid the numerous potholes we came to while Mike somehow managed to hit almost every one.

After a few minutes of this without an explosion, I began to relax a little, allowing me the time to curse myself for letting events spiral out of my control. After another twenty minutes, we pulled up on the pier. I immediately made my way up the gangway and down to my cabin. I didn't want anything further to do with the cases of explosives we'd brought on board.

As I sat on my bunk, I was relieved to still be alive and exhausted. Where Mike and Chris ended up storing the dynamite, I didn't know or care. If we hadn't blown ourselves up on the way back bouncing down that dirt road, I figured we'd be OK at least until they tried to set them off. That wouldn't be for a day or two, and I had to get a few hours' sleep before I started my sixteen. If I had known what lay ahead when I awoke, I would have used every minute of the eight hours I had off to sleep. I wouldn't make that mistake again.

Because the *Royal Enterprise* was a processor as well as a catcher, it needed a lot of salt. The salt was used in the cooking and freezing process, so it used thousands of pounds of it. The trucks delivering that salt in the form of fifty-pound bags were just arriving as I came onto deck to start my first sixteen-hour shift in port.

Pallets holding fifty-pound bags were lifted out of the trucks using forklifts and set into position on the dock next to the ship so they could be lifted by the ship's crane onto a clear space up on the third deck of boat near the bow. From there a human chain was used to take the bags off the pallets one at a time and move them to the storage compartment where they would be stored and retrieved during our trip.

As life usually arranges things, the pallets did not end up right next to the compartment where they were to be stored. Instead our human chain extended from the third deck down to the second deck then along a walkway to a compartment near midship. There they would be stacked eight feet high to the ceiling, eventually filling the compartment full. To get them to the second deck, it made sense that it was easier to lower the fifty-pound bags down from the third deck using gravity than it would to lift them by hand from the first deck.

So far that sounded reasonable to me until I found out that using gravity meant dropping the bags from the third deck into the arms of a person standing on the second deck from a height of about ten feet and that person was going to be me. This meant that for many hours to come, I would be catching hundreds of fifty-pound bags of salt being dropped to me from ten feet high and passing them along the human chain.

It didn't take a rocket scientist to understand that this was the worst place to be in the chain and that it was no accident that I ended up there. Remember that contract I signed to be a crewman on this voyage? Well, if you wanted to be part of the crew, there was a series of initiations for a greenhorn to pass first as the crew would want to know if you had what it was going to take to stand with them on deck out at sea when the going got tough. This provided the first opportunity to do that before we got underway.

Out there they say attitude is everything. I'd be watched closely to see if I indeed had the right attitude. None of this was explained to me by anyone, of course; either I'd pick up on what was going on or I wouldn't. Fortunately I'd been around the block once or twice in my short life, so I figured out what was happening pretty quickly.

The only question was, would I be able to endure the excruciating work that lay ahead?

The onloading of salt began, and the bags started down the line. Everyone settled into a rhythm. It didn't take long for the pain to begin; minutes passed into hours as I was pounded by an endless barrage of bags being dropped into my aching arms. I actually couldn't physically catch fifty pounds with just my arms from that height for long. I found if I lifted my leg and used my thigh under my arms, it gave more support. This really worked well and made it possible to keep up the grueling pace.

Nevertheless as the hours passed, the muscle pain in my back and arms was excruciating, and I found myself thinking of ways I could find an acceptable excuse to take a break. I realized that I was going to be working with these guys for months out in the middle of nowhere. Gaining and keeping their respect was everything if I was going to succeed on this voyage. I decided that I'd wait for someone else to take the first break. Surely it wouldn't be long now.

Time passed. The bags kept coming one after another. *Damn it, when will someone call for a break?* I told myself. All I needed was a few minutes rest and then I'd be OK. This was a lie; I knew that if I was able to stop that moment it would take days for me to recover. I began to get pissed off. I noticed that my anger was giving me more strength. I began to focus my anger on each bag as it dropped into my arms, and I passed it on. I had learned long ago that the mind quits long before the body will.

I began to push through my mental fatigue by using my anger to tell myself I wasn't going to allow these bags of salt to defeat me. *Who the hell were these guys anyway?* I'd never witnessed this level of human endurance before. *What have I got myself into?*

After six straight hours, a voice rang out from the upper deck, "Last bags on their way."

By this point, I was in a numbed state of awareness, and the words kind of drifted over me without really registering. A minute or two later, I turned to catch the next bag, and nothing happened. I looked up to see Mike, the deck boss, leaning over the rail of the deck above me with a huge smile on his face. "That's it, Doc. Head on down to the galley. We're going to take a break for a while. I'll see you down there in a while."

That was definitely one of, if not the most, difficult things I'd ever done in my life. A rush of absolute relief passed through me as I realized we were really finished with the salt. I slowly made my way down to the galley as a growing feeling of accomplishment swelled up inside me. I'd done it.

We had a chance to heat frozen burritos in a microwave and had about fifteen minutes to eat them before we went back to work. After another six straight hours of loading cases of food and stacks of frozen bait, I finished the rest of my shift. After twelve hours of backbreaking work, eating only two frozen burritos, I was famished. I was too tired and delirious to eat and immediately went to my room and collapsed in my bunk, falling asleep the instant my head hit the pillow.

When I woke up, I could feel the gentle motion of the boat rolling on water and hear the engines running with a steady muffled roar. I realized that we were underway. As I rolled out of my bunk, I almost fell to the deck as my body was almost completely paralyzed. Any movement brought intense pain as my muscles screamed to be left alone. I noticed large black and blue bruises on the front of my thighs where hundreds of salt bags had landed the night before. It took all my effort to get dressed and waddle out on deck.

There was a buzz of excitement on deck. It took me a moment to see that preparations were underway to set off the dynamite we'd found the other day. Who said there was no time for a little fun? Every muscle, tendon, and ligament ached to the point I literally could hardly move. I was too tired to care any more about any danger. Anyway it was far too late to do anything about it. I might as well find a good vantage point and watch the festivities.

The pot launcher was a metal platform set on the rail of the ship. It used hydraulic lifts that change the angle of the platform. It could be lifted to tilt so the crab pot will slide off it into the ocean or be tilted back toward the deck to shake out the crab captured inside onto the sorting table. The platform had a set of hooks that held the pot in place. They could be retracted to allow the pot to slide off the ramp when the pots were ready to be set. That day the launcher was going to be used to drop a pallet with a case of dynamite, with a lit fuse stuck in one end, over the side of the boat and explode behind us.

Mike and Dave were in charge of the operation, and everyone was giddy with excitement. As for myself, I'd had the unique experience of working on an ambulance for over the last year and had spent my days treating the injured and seeing people dead from doing things a lot less stupid than this. So I was a little more sensitive to the potential danger we all were in, which tended to temper my excitement level. I watched in fascination as several crew members laid out a pallet on the launcher while Mike set the case of dynamite in place. A roll of duct tape was produced, and the case was taped down to the pallet

Satisfied the case was held in place sufficiently, Mike pulled out a fuse from his coat pocket and stuck it into the end of a single stick of dynamite he held in his hand. The detonators needed an electric charge to set them off. The old-fashioned fuses only needed heat. Chris then approached with a lit cigarette lighter which he touched to the end of the fuse. It ignited and began to burn. Mike unflinchingly set the stick with the lit fuse back into the case of forty-nine sticks of explosives, stepped back, and gave the signal to launch the case overboard.

As the hooks retracted, the pallet slid smoothly off the launcher and splashed into the sea. As soon as it did, everyone ran to prearranged positions to get a view at the massive explosion that would occur at any moment. It was another bright sunny day, and visibility was perfect with calm seas. The *Royal Enterprise* cruised on at about twelve knots or approximately fourteen an hour.

I wondered if Mike and Dave had tested to see how long it took a fuse to burn down to the end. Semiresigned to death in my currently miserable state, I waited in anticipation with the rest of the crew. Seconds ticked off as the pallet fell off our stern in our wake. A hundred yards, then two hundred, and after several minutes, the pallet was just a speck disappearing behind us. Some crew members produced binoculars determined to see the explosion.

Finally it was apparent to everyone that the attempt was a failure. "Not to worry," came a shout from Dave, "we still have another case of dynamite. We'll try it again."

A burst of activity ensued as another pallet appeared, and the process was repeated. This time however, Mike decided to increase the odds of success. He pulled out a fuse from one coat pocket and a pocket knife from the other and proceeded to cut the fuse in half before placing it into the end of a stick of dynamite. The level of internalized excitement raised several notches in everyone as they witnessed this act of determination by Mike. I shook my head in disbelief.

The fuse was lit, and the pallet sent overboard. As before, the pallet mercifully passed to our stern without blowing the ship out of the water and drifted farther and farther behind us as the tension mounted with each passing moment. As before, first seconds and then minutes passed without anything happening.

By now even I was strangely disappointed as slowly it became clear the venture was a failure. With the muffled voices of disappointment mingling with the sea breeze, everyone began to return to their regular duties. I wondered if I was the only one concerned that we had left two pallets of dynamite floating in the sea lanes to Dutch. I guessed if we managed to sink an unsuspecting vessel that had the misfortune of running into one of those pallets in the middle of the night, we'd hear about it over the radio.

That concern quickly passed as I struggled to get my body to move again so I could get though another torturous day that was surely before me.

I did take a moment to look out to sea from the starboard rail and peer to the distant horizon. Our course was due east. We were just north of the Aleutian Island chain. Our next stop was the Russian port city of Petropavlovsk (the city of Peter and Paul), Kamchatka. This was the most important city on the Kamchatka Peninsula. It was founded by Vitus Bering himself in 1740 when he finally arrived at Avacha Bay after his eight-year journey from St. Petersburg. Like Commander Bering, my personal voyage of discovery had finally begun. I was then literally sailing in Bering's wake.

It's only in adventure that some people succeed in knowing themselves, in finding themselves.

—Andre Gide

Chapter 7

In Bering's Wake

Alaid Volcano, Kamchatka

It was a four-day voyage to the Kamchatka Peninsula where we were scheduled to pick up three Russian fishery observers. The first night out of Dutch, we went on four-hour wheel-watch shifts at night.

I was given a lesson on chart reading and navigation so I could fill one of the four-hour slots during the night on our way across the Bering Sea. That was how I found myself at the helm of a 110-foot ship as it plowed its way through the night bound for Siberia. Gone were the days of the ship's wheel and compass I had learned in the Coast Guard decades before. These days the ship could be steered by a knob on a console, and the compass had been replaced with satellite GPS. Although technology had changed, being at the helm of a ship on the open ocean was still quite a thrill, with the lives of everyone on board your responsibility.

There's a swivel chair bolted to the deck where you can sit behind a console. You have a commanding view overlooking the bow and the sea beyond. A radar screen with its eerie green light is in front of you on the console, illuminating the otherwise dark wheelhouse. The radar can show you what's around you in a twenty-mile circle. The radio waves can reflect back off the top of waves if the seas are high enough and produce a sparkling of lights on the screen.

No responsible sailor will trust his life to radar 100 percent, so the hours are spent whether day or night scanning the horizon for anything that might ruin your life if you happened to run into it. However tempting it becomes to doze off for a moment or two while all alone in the middle of the night staring out into empty space, any man with half a brain will constantly remind himself of the disaster that awaits any fool who dares.

On the morning of the third day, our course put us sailing past Bering Island. I first observed the island on the boat's radar screen in the wheelhouse. The early morning was very grey and overcast with banks of fog and rain. There was little chance to see anything in these conditions; besides, we were about five miles south of the island as well.

Despite the dismal conditions, at one point while passing the island, its gloomy grey silhouette emerged out of the mist on our horizon. I grabbed a pair of binoculars off the radar console and peered out at the island. It appeared like a grey ghost in an unearthly dream. The feeling of absolute isolation and despair welled up inside me as I thought of Captain Bering and his crew stranded there for months through the winter of 1741-1742. For a few minutes, I got a feeling of the utter loneliness they must have felt before the island vanished behind a fog bank and was gone.

By the next morning, we had covered the three hundred miles or so from Bering Island to the Kamchatka coast outside the entrance to Avacha Bay. It had taken the surviving crew of Bering's expedition fourteen days to cover the same distance. Unlike the day before, that morning was crystal clear; the towering volcanoes surrounding Petropavlovsk, covered in snow, stood out brilliantly against the beautiful sky blue horizon. Koryakskaya, the largest, is 11,339 feet high.

We were restricted from entering the bay and docking at Petropavlovsk due to the fact that Rybachiy Nuclear Submarine Base, Russia's largest, was located in the bay. However friendly the relationship had become between the United States and the Soviet Union, they certainly hadn't become that friendly. However, shortly after we had dropped our anchor, we were treated to a rare sight that few people anywhere have seen, a Soviet nuclear-powered submarine on the surface entering the bay in broad daylight.

Russian nuclear sub *Boomer* entering Avacha Bay

Later in the afternoon, a small boat appeared in the distance heading our way. As it got closer, we were told that was the boat carrying the biologists we had come for, and most of the crew gathered on the starboard rail to get a look. The vessel was about thirty feet long and resembled a cross between a tugboat and a ride at Disney World. It nudged up to our side bow first, and the three observers jumped on board followed by their gear that was unceremoniously tossed over to our boat. Immediately after the Russians were on board, the tug pulled away. We weighed anchor and set sail.

Our course was south by southeast following the coastline of the massive peninsula. Below us was the Kuril Trench with a depth of over twenty-six thousand feet of water. This is where two tectonic plates collided together, forcing one down underneath the other, forming the deep trench and the massive amount of volcanic activity that had formed the Kamchatka Peninsula. Throughout the day as we sailed on, the towering peaks of huge volcanoes followed us in an awesome procession.

We made our turn at the tip of the peninsula and made our way through the Kuril Straits between Cape Lopatka and Shumshu Island. Soon the Alaid Volcano loomed on the horizon. This island volcano rises up from the sea bottom 9,840 feet then from sea level another 7,674 feet. A dirty grey plume of smoke and ash rose out of its cone and drifted off over the western horizon like an ancient primal finger pointing out our way to the unknown sea beyond.

As we entered the Sea of Okhotsk, I was busy working in the processing area helping the engineers put the final touches on the equipment we'd use to process our catch. Justin, our interpreter, came in and said I was needed in the galley. Apparently my first medical case had arrived

He explained to me as we made our way to the galley that the deckhand Kevin had part of his molar break off while eating and was in excruciating pain. Dentistry, great! Now I was a dentist. We quickly arrived to find Kevin, a full-grown, very rugged man, in tears, moaning and withering around uncontrollably, in pain from the exposed nerves.

"Doc, for Christ's sake, do something. I can't take this pain," he said as I came in close to get a look in his mouth. He handed me the chunk of tooth that had broken off as he continued to squirm and moan.

I took a good look at the piece of tooth and then peered into Kevin's mouth. I quickly learned that in situations where you had no idea what you were doing it was important to act like you did. This bought the critical time to figure something out that might work, thus saving face and your job.

The first thing was to get his pain under control. I turned to Justin and asked him to get my medical bag. He soon returned, and I decided to use both ibuprofen orally, 800 mg, and prepare an injection of lidocaine. The ibuprofen would take twenty minutes to take effect but hopefully would stop the pain for hours; the lidocaine would act immediately, enabling me to try and fix his tooth.

There are few circumstances more dreaded than to have a dental emergency at sea. Everyone instinctively knows you're in deep shit. The world of dentistry to a sailor is a strange and mysterious one, much more so than to land-dwelling folks for reasons I've never come to understand. Perhaps because being thousands of miles from civilization in a slow-moving boat that in the best of conditions will take days or weeks to return to a port, the thought of dealing with the unique pain levels that a tooth can bring to bear on a man is terrifying. I've seen it reduce the largest, strongest, toughest man to his knees, crying like a child for his mother.

So when I produced a long needle on the end of a syringe, Kevin barely flinched. Once he understood that this needle offered him his only chance at salvation from his current ordeal, he became more than willing to allow me to inject the medication around his fractured tooth into his gums. Nevertheless I was really glad he was unaware that it was my first time doing anything like this before.

Apparently I was hitting the right places for almost immediately he began to calm down and relax as the medication blocked the pain receptors to his brain. A smile slowly grew on his face as he became convinced this was working. At that moment, I became a hero as the rest of the crew let out murmurs of approval and delight at the apparent magic I had just performed.

Then for the hard part. I knew this was just temporary, and if I did not come up with a successful plan immediately, this could significantly delay our voyage. I had temporary filling epoxy in my bag, but that would not hold his tooth together.

I made Kevin comfortable in a bunk and told him I'd be right back, everything was under control, and I'd take care of this problem. I stepped in the ship's office, shut the door, and sat down. Alone for the moment, I let out a deep sigh and slumped over in the chair. *Think!* I needed something that would glue the broken chunk of tooth back in place.

Upon my examination, I saw that the piece fit like a puzzle neatly back against the remaining tooth. I just needed something that would hold it in place until we returned to the United States.

I sat up and leaned back in my chair. My mind went kind of blank as I began to slowly look around at my surroundings in the office. A typical office with all the regular paraphernalia was laid out on the desk: a stapler, pens, stacks of paper, a bottle of Wite-Out, a computer, and a tube of superglue. *A tube of superglue?* I leaned over and picked up the small tube of glue. *We've all seen the commercials, right? Superglue will glue anything!*

What I was thinking at that moment was crazy, or was it? I'd just taken a look at the directions for use on the back of the tube: will glue wood, glass, stone, ceramic, metal, and almost everything; make sure surface to be glued is clean and dry. As I read the directions, the more convinced I was this might work. Besides, I was running out of ideas and time.

"What the hell," I said out loud. "What do I have to lose?"

With that I grabbed the tube of superglue and went back to where Kevin was resting. "OK, let's get this over with," I said in a reassuring tone.

I had Kevin gargle with mouthwash; while he was doing that, I dropped the tooth fragment into a pan of alcohol. I had Kevin then sit in a chair and tilt his back. I packed cotton balls between his cheek and gums, upper and lower, on both sides of his mouth. If this was going to work, his mouth had to be completely dry.

With his head tilted back and his eyes closed (perfect), I explained to him that I had some dental glue I hoped would hold the broken piece in place until we got back home. I added as a way out that the glue had been in the medical bag for what appeared to be years, and I wasn't sure it was still good.

"OK, hold still while I put the fragment in place." With that I put one drop of superglue on the fragment, reached into his open mouth, and set the piece back into position. It fit back in place perfectly. I wiped the excess glue off with my gloved finger and stepped back.

"Hold still now for just a minute longer. I know it's uncomfortable with all those cotton balls in your mouth, but it will just be a minute," I said, crossing my fingers. After a minute, I removed all the cotton balls and said, "How does it feel?"

Kevin sat up, moved his jaw around, and opened and shut his mouth a few times. Finally satisfied, he looked at me and said, "Feels good, Doc. I think you did it."

"Open one more time," I replied. I took another look using a dental mirror to get a good view. Damn, it was holding. It looked great. "OK, here's the deal," I explained. "Baby that side of your mouth as much as possible, try to chew on the other side only, and brush very lightly over that tooth, understand?"

"Yeah, Doc, I got it."

With that he got up, and I followed him back to the galley where some of the crew waited to see the outcome. Handshakes and pats on the back followed as the word spread that I had been successful. I went back to work in the processing compartment, although every day we were at sea, I worried if the glue would hold. Kevin never had any trouble with that tooth the rest of our voyage. I had a very steep learning curve to overcome, but I was learning.

On the stack, *Royal Enterprise*, Sea of Okhotsk, 1991

The weather was grey, cloudy, with wind and rain. The time had come for our crabbing operations to begin. When we were in Dutch Harbor, we had loaded three hundred crab pots on the stern of the *Royal Enterprise*. They were stacked side by side in rows and on top of each other, rising thirty feet high or three stories. They were tied together individually with pieces of nylon rope about three feet long, each pot tied to the one beside it and to the one above and below on the upper stacks.

Then as the ship's crane began to lift them from the stack and prepare them to be dropped overboard, the crew had to untie all these hundreds of ropes as each pot became exposed and was ready to be moved. Being part of the crew, I joined in and climbed up to the top of the stack and found a spot to fit in and began the process of unlashing the pots.

I quickly realized that this was very dangerous work. The ship was rolling side to side, and I was standing on metal railings of the frames of the pots with wet boots forty feet above the ocean whose temperature hovered at about thirty-eight degrees. As each pot was lifted from the stack in the rolling seas, the eight-hundred-pound pots swung back and forth seemingly determined to sweep all of us off into the sea.

This was life-and-death work where you had to keep your head on a swivel at all times; a moment's lapse of attention could be fatal. From thereon out, this was to be the norm, and my responsibility on this voyage became crystal clear. So important was my presence on the ship that after about two hours on the stack, the captain happened to recognize me through all my rain gear and came out from the wheelhouse shouting for the crew to get me off the stack.

"Doc, get your ass off there. Are you trying to get yourself killed, for Christ's sake? What will we do if you get hurt?" he shouted. "Find something else safer for him to do, Mike, for Christ's sake," he continued.

I looked over to the others near me on the stack to see their reaction to the order; they each looked at me and shrugged the shoulders as if to say, you tried, man, that's what counts. I slowly made my way down to the main deck a bit embarrassed and disappointed as well. I liked doing dangerous things. It made me feel alive and put me in that exact moment of my life.

Mike came over and said, "Good work up there. Sorry, go into the processing room and help John get things squared away in there, OK?"

"Yeah, sure, Mike," I replied and went inside for the rest of our shift.

That day was our first twenty on and four off schedule; from then on, operations would continue around the clock seven days a week. The way it worked, you worked a minimum of twenty hours and at some unknown time to you, you'd be approached by the deck boss and told to take your four hours off.

Normally pots are individually dropped overboard each with its own buoy attached for future pickup. On that trip, we were going to be what was called long lining where a string of thirty pots are tied to one line with a buoy attached at one end of the string and one at the other end. The pots are stacked on deck in a line, and the buoy at one end of the line is tossed off the stern along with the coils of line that connect all the pots. As the ship moves forward, the pots are pulled off the stern one after the other until the buoy at the far end is thrown over last.

The result is a two-mile-long line of pots resting on the ocean floor, each several hundred feet apart. After enough time for them to hopefully fill with crab, usually twenty-four hours, the boat returns to one end of the line. The buoy is retrieved and starts the labor-intensive job of raising each pot in line, emptying and sorting the crab, rebaiting the now-empty pot, and dropping it back over the side just in time to bring up the next pot and repeat the process over and over and over again around the clock.

The only break was around every six hours. You'd be told you had fifteen minutes to go to the galley and get something to eat. Since we had no cook, this meant microwaving a frozen burrito, usually burning the hell out of the inside of your mouth eating it before it cooled from the lava state, and rushing back out on deck to continue on. The only other time during your twenty-hour shift to take a break was when we were between strings and were heading for another line of pots a few miles or so away.

The lonely sea

Usually it was about a half hour to the next string, and on rare occasions, it might be longer. In any case, those of us on deck would immediately go to the gear room right off the main deck and collapse on the floor with all our wet stinking gear on and fall straight to sleep, too totally exhausted to care about anything else in the entire world.

The *Royal Enterprise* was also a processor, so the backbreaking work of bringing the crab to the surface was only half the job. When the hopper was full on deck with king crab, the processing would begin. A door could be opened from inside the processing area, enabling the crab to be brought into the butchering line; and the work of butchering, cooking, freezing, and casing the crab then would take place. The finished product of a ninety-five-pound case of frozen crab was then stacked into an elevator that lowered down one deck to the freezer hold. There, usually two men worked twenty-hour shifts stacking hundreds of ninety-five-pound cases of crab in thirty-degrees-below-zero temperatures.

Once the whole process of setting the pots and retrieving them then resetting and processing the catch got into full swing, the absolutely backbreaking nightmare grind began. Very few people in Western society can fully understand the level of suffering and pain that men endure while working these operations.

For me, this was a level of work I had never experienced before and believed did not exist anymore in the twentieth century. Except for Justin, our interpreter, and I, the rest of the crew took it in stride and seemed immune to the torture that I'm sure all of us were feeling.

These guys were a different breed of men. The kind of men I'd read about in books that lived a hundred years or more ago. It never occurred to me that somewhere in the world today their kind still existed. Somehow I had not only found they did indeed still exist, but by some strange fate I had put myself into a position to somehow equal their incredible feats of strength and endurance. It was apparent from the get-go that there was no way out of this. If I could have quit I would have, but being on a small boat in the middle of a sea off the coast of Siberia made that option impossible.

The only way out was through. I had unwittingly set myself up for the greatest physical and mental challenge of my life, and there was nothing I could do to change this fact. Luckily for me, I had skirted this world before in other experiences in my life.

I began to draw upon some of the lessons I had learned from those. The most important one of these lessons was that the mind gives up long before the body. The level of human strength is 99 percent mental. Just believing this doesn't make anything any easier, but it gives you a place to start the minute-by-minute, day-by-day struggle you're involved in. It gives you an anchor in which to hold yourself in place against the waves of anguish and despair that constantly break over you during your ordeal.

This is the one thing I had that my closest friend on the boat, Justin, did not. The difference of understanding this seemingly minor truth that the mind controls the body, and never showing weakness in front of men like these under any circumstances, would begin to play itself out in dramatic fashion in the days to come.

It was late September by now. The days grew shorter and with this the wind shifted to the north, bringing down cold Arctic air. The seas began to grow more agitated as the strength of the northern wind grew.

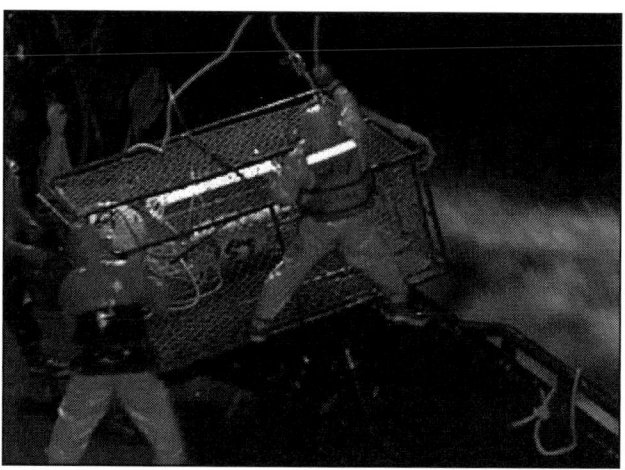

Launching a pot, *Royal Enterprise*, 1991

During the winter months, the Sea of Okhotsk is covered with ice. Only the stoutest icebreakers sail her then. We needed to catch our quota as fast as possible and retreat from this sea as soon as we could. We had a long way to go, and the only way to succeed was by superhuman will and brute strength. Our fishing operations would continue 24/7 in all weather conditions until we had accomplished our mission.

Being the new guy, I was put in the baiting station which was the worst job on deck. The bait was frozen herring and frozen meat scraps from slaughterhouses, in forty-pound blocks. On deck, mounted on the bulkhead, was a primitive but effective grinder. It ate the blocks of frozen bait without any effort and spit out the disgusting mess into a large, heavy-duty plastic tote.

From there you'd stuff the ground-up meat into large plastic jars that had holes punched throughout the containers; they were joined together in bunches of three held together by large D-ring-style carabiner hooks. After they were filled, they were run over to a crab pot that had been staged on the launcher; and climbing inside the pot on your back, you had to lift the twenty-pound jars and clip them on the netting on the top section of the pot.

This process would continue without letup as long as pots were being launched. The pace was grueling, and usually it was difficult to keep up even when you worked as fast as you could. It only took twenty minutes before you were exhausted, and not long after that, your hands continually in contact with frozen bait became frozen themselves even while wearing rubber gloves with liners. Lying on your back in the pot and trying to lift the jars into place worked a set of muscles on the back side of your arms and shoulders that you never had really used before, and it only took baiting a dozen pots before this became extremely painful.

This was the most dangerous job on the boat; as the ship listed and large waves made their way over the deck, it was quite possible for them to wash the pot off the launcher overboard into the icy waters. It had happened many times before I had arrived out there, and it was one of the greatest fears for a crabber to be trapped inside a crab pot as it plunged to the depths. Needless to say, this was always on your mind during the endless agonizing hours you were climbing into the pots. If there is a hell that exists anywhere in our universe, I was convinced then that was what a person would suffer there, baiting crab pots endlessly.

Justin was in his early twenties on this voyage. His job was to be our interpreter. Compared to the other crewmen, he was slight of build, around five feet, eight inches tall, and maybe 160 pounds. He was from Portland, a student at one of Oregon's universities, studying Russian. He was offered the same deal as I, which was to sign on as a crew member. Like me, he didn't have a clue what he was getting into and was more out of his league out there than I was.

Justin and I were just regular, middle-class twentieth-century guys. We were not cut from the same fabric as our fellow crewmates. Both of us were looked at as outsiders, land lovers, and well, pussies. These guys were a tough bunch. They had to be, to endure the incredible hardships this life at sea demanded. Therein was the difference that separated us from them. They chose to live this life after knowing full well what it took to survive. Justin and I, on the other hand, had ended up there through sheer ignorance of what we were getting ourselves into. By that point in the voyage, both of us realized we wouldn't be signing up to do this again. Already we were both just figuring out how we'd make it through the day, let alone returning for a full voyage in the future.

The daily grind continued without letup. I was so sore and miserable, words cannot describe it. I was borderline seasick all the time; and on occasion, depending on the motion of the sea or the stench of the rotten crab shells and debris scattered on the processing floor, completely seasick, retching my empty guts out while continuing to work twenty-hour shifts. Out here there are no sick days or breaks for being sick or tired. Everyone is expected to work a full shift every day, the only exception being near death or death itself. None of us knew one of the rare opportunities for a break was quickly approaching.

Look for me in the whirlwind of the storm.

—Marcus Garvey

Chapter 8

The Wave

Wave over the *Royal Enterprise*, 1991

One day the sea had built into what I can best describe as what a farmer's field looks like. You've seen the long rows of dirt mounded up with the valleys in between. That day the sea was like that, with the rolling waves twenty feet high and hundred feet wide, the valleys in between were a hundred feet wide.

The way the string of pots being brought up were laid out on the sea bottom, the *Royal Enterprise* had to keep on a course that put us sideways to the oncoming rollers. The desired position for a sea like this was to approach the wave's bow first, slicing through the wall of water. Unable to maneuver in that way, we were forced to come into the massive rollers broadside, riding up one side of the mountain of water and then sliding off the other side into the trough below.

With deck operations taking place on the exposed deck, the situation had become a lot more dangerous than normal. Timing then became the name of the game. All the work and maneuvering of heavy pots took place on the rail of the boat. A week earlier, I had stepped out on deck from the processing plant just as another pot full of crab had snapped from the line, sending it to the bottom.

George, who had been working the controls that raised the pots from the bottom, had snapped the line on several pots earlier. As the pots came up, you could see them in the crystal-clear water when they reached about thirty feet from the surface. From there you would wait until the pot turned flush with the hull then bring it up to the surface, ensuring it wouldn't hit the bottom of the hull, snapping the line. After the third pot was sent to the bottom, George was unceremoniously dragged from the controls as those on deck cursed him with every word in the book. Mike saw me standing there and made the comment, "I think Doc could do a better job on the rail as George."

There was a moment of silence as everyone on deck came to the same conclusion. "Hey, why not train Doc to do the job. He can't be any worse," Kevin shouted out.

That's how I came to work the winch controls that were mounted on the railing of the deck and required you to lean over the railing and look down into the ocean to see the pot's position as it comes up. As the boat slid off the top of a roller and plunged into the trough below, the broadside position of the ship hitting the water sent up huge walls of water up and over the deck and everyone on it.

The right time to bring up the eight-hundred-pound crab pot on deck was critical then. We had developed our timing to do this successfully, and operations continued with a steady rhythm. It meant however that as each wave crashed onto the deck, all of us working had to hold on to something bolted down to the deck to keep from being swept overboard. I ducked straight down, grabbing on to the bottom of the metal support post for the upper wing deck. It was like having a swimming pool dumped on you every five minutes and being in a washing machine at the same time. Several times during the night, I'd been knocked on my ass and washed across the deck because I'd been so focused on looking down into the sea at the pot coming to the surface I hadn't seen the wall of water heading for the ship.

We had been working like this for going on seventeen hours. We were all far beyond exhausted, freezing cold, and wet. Moving robotically in a stupor, we struggled to keep the mental edge you needed to stay alive in conditions like this. All kinds of moving heavy machinery, tons of ice-cold water, and a heavily listing deck added up to trouble.

Another wall of water shot up as the *Royal Enterprise* came crashing down off another roller. We all dived for our prearranged positions to hold on. A sixty-foot-long, twenty-foot-high wall of green water rose up over the rail as the familiar warning cry, "Wave!" was shouted out. Tons of water filled the deck four feet deep as we all held our breath and waited for the water to recede and return to the sea. As we staggered to our feet, all our eyes seemed to be drawn to a point on deck that presented one of the most bizarre sights any of us had witnessed.

Justin was lying on his back, flopping around like a fish out of water with a five-hundred-pound stainless steel sorting table lying on its side across his chest. The captain immediately throttled back on the engines as we on deck stood frozen at the impossible sight before us. After a moment of shock, we all sprang into action.

First thing was to lift the massive table off Justin. Clumsily at first, two men tried to lift one end as several more of us tried to lift the other at the same time. It instantly was clear the table was too heavy to try and lift the whole thing at once. Mike, the deck boss, quickly took control of the momentary confusion.

"Goddamnit!" he shouted. "Everyone get on one end and lift together. On three, ready, one, two, three, lift!" With everyone straining, the end of the table lifted just enough for Justin to be pulled out from under it.

The tension in the air was thick, it was a miracle he was still alive. Normally I'd do a quick exam before moving a patient, but there was no time for that now. Another wave was already on its way, and Justin needed to be moved immediately. One man was under each arm, and one lifted his legs, and he was quickly carried to the galley.

A thousand different emotions crossed through my mind as I realized that it would be up to me to take control of the situation. Although I had learned long ago how to control the panic and fear that sets in during an emergency call after working the big city streets of Seattle answering hundreds of 911 calls. This was my first real life threatening emergency at sea; the difference now was that I was completely alone. No doctors, nurses, or even a hospital just hundreds of miles of empty ocean. As Justin was being carried off the deck it took all the mental strength I had to keep the fear which felt like an angry tiger clawing at my brain locked in its cage.

Justin was laid out on his back on the galley floor. Those who had carried him stepped back to allow me through. I knelt down next to him and began to ask him how he felt and where it hurt while I stripped him of his rain gear and underclothes. I felt his chest for broken ribs, asking him if he could breathe OK. His eyes were as big as plates as he followed my exam with as much curiosity as I had. I had expected the worst: crushed ribs, ruptured spleen, perforated lungs, and eventual death.

Slowly it became clear as I ran my hands over his body, prodding here and pressing there, that other than a few bruises on his chest, he had suffered no visible injuries. Five hundred pounds dropped on a human chest even from only a foot in height was capable of serious injury. Crush syndrome occurs when internal organs are compressed, and when the pressure is relaxed on them, toxins are released into the bloodstream that can bring on organ failure, usually to the kidneys first then liver and so on and can lead to death. The symptoms of crush syndrome do not appear right away and can take hours to be noticed without an MRI or CAT scan.

Apparently, after a lot of discussion with other members of the crew, our conclusion of what had happened was that the table was lifted off its holding brackets, floated across the deck, and as the water receded, was gently placed down on Justin's chest as he was being washed across the deck after losing his grip, quite possibly keeping him from being carried overboard. Was it a miracle? None of us could say. It certainly was a million-to-one event; a hundred lifetimes at sea and you would never witness something so strange, and yet it happened right before our eyes as smooth as silk.

Justin was extremely sore, making it difficult for him to move I had no way of assessing internal injuries other than to wait and see if any negative symptoms developed over a period of time. I felt that a few hours of observation was wise before he returned to working on deck. That idea was dismissed by Mike and the rest of the crew who only went by what they saw and that was Justin looked fine.

I had been trained to err on the side of caution. Someone's life was potentially at stake. Operations on deck could continue without Justin especially for just a few hours longer. So I stood my ground and insisted we wait a few hours for observation before he went back to work. Reluctantly Mike gave in, and Justin was given two hours off.

I had no idea what consequences this decision would have for Justin in the near future. When he did finally return to work a few hours later, it quickly became clear the crew had turned on Justin. He was treated with disdain and disrespect throughout his shift on deck, much to his dismay and mine.

Crabbing operations were in full swing now. Our days were spent pulling and dropping pots and processing our catch. After approximately twenty hours, the deck boss would tap you on the shoulder and tell you to be back to work in four hours. Unless you dropped your rain gear in the gear room and went right to bed, you ended up getting about three hours of sleep in twenty-four. When you were woken up, you were so sore and tired that by the time you got up, had a cup of coffee, and got your gear on, a half hour had passed. The same was true when you were relieved after a twenty-hour shift. You were usually hungry and filthy. If you stopped to eat or clean up at all, a half hour could pass before you knew it. As a result in the desperate attempt to get as much sleep as we could we began to eat far less than we should have. Taking the time to take a shower or clean our clothes quickly became a luxury none of us could afford. The result was we all began to lose weight and smell terrible. It was difficult to enter any room on the boat for the thick foul order that instantly assaulted our senses.

It didn't take many days like this to start to grind you into a staggering stupor. Throughout the long day, Mike or another senior crew man would stand over you literally screaming at the top of their lungs for you to hurry up and to work harder. The noise level was ear shattering, forcing me at least to wear earplugs and headphone ear protectors against the sound level from all the machinery, engines, hydraulics from the crane, not to mention the stereo music system rigged up by some of the crew, blasting out heavy metal music at sonic boom levels to be heard over all the rest of the noise.

The decibels were so high that not wearing both kinds of ear protectors felt like a knitting needle was being pushed through your ear. The pain was unbearable. The endless backbreaking labor, the ear-piercing noise, the stress of being verbally pushed to work as hard as possible the entire time as well as being cold, hungry, and seasick put me in a state of shock and bewilderment.

Pacing myself was the only way I quickly realized I could make it through the day. So began the delicate art of pacing myself just enough as to not look too obvious, which would immediately bring down the wrath of whoever was in charge at the time.

This crew had an ingenious although devious method of punishment for any perceived slacking. It was called "sharping." If, after several warnings to pick up the pace of work did not bring the desired results, you were informed that you had been sharped. This was reducing your time off by an hour each time you were seen to not be pulling your weight. You can imagine that the most valuable thing in our entire world by that time was sleep. The idea of taking away any of the three hours we were getting then was unimaginable.

But if I had any ideas of quitting, and I did about every five minutes throughout the day, they slowly melted away due to the one inescapable fact: it was impossible to quit. Where would you go? We were in the middle of the Sea of Okhotsk off the coast of Siberia. In your wildest imagination, one would be hard-pressed to come up with a place more isolated or far away from home than where we were then. Oh, yeah, I almost forgot. If you quit in the middle of a voyage, you wouldn't get paid for all the time you worked up till then. Your percentage of earnings would be divided up among the rest of the crew. As much pain as one could suffer, giving up your pay might be something you'd consider but there was one other insurmountable problem, there was nowhere to go after you quit. Like being trapped in a nightmare you'd be stuck on the boat the rest of the trip, another four weeks no doubt locked in your room surrounded by large angry men who had nothing but contempt for you. The thought of ending up in these circumstances was worse than working your way through the voyage.

Fortunately for me, I could muster the extra effort at the right time, and I stayed alert to my surroundings for when I might be able to let up just a little to husband my limited energy resources. Justin was not as fortunate and simply, as time went on, became utterly exhausted. The crew was relentlessly teasing and taunting Justin throughout the miserable shifts. They looked for the slightest sign of weakness in both of us and like sharks sensing blood, moved in for the kill. Even after repeated threats of being sharped, Justin could not find the strength to increase his output. Each day the crew became more and more abusive toward him, pulling cruel practical jokes that humiliated him and making it obvious they were disliking him more and more with each passing day.

Somehow I managed to find the energy to keep them at bay since they respected strength. I made every effort to show them I had what it took to be their equal. Finally the unthinkable happened, and one afternoon, Justin was sharped. His shift was now twenty-one hours on and three off. I'll never forget the hollowed look in his eyes as he put his head down and continued on with his hopeless task.

Not long after, I was told I was relieved and immediately went to my bunk and fell into a deep sleep only to be awakened an hour later by the intense numbness in both of my arms from my shoulders to my fingertips. This is caused by a condition called tendinitis, after 20 hours of hard labor during sleep your muscles would swell cutting off the circulation to your arms. The only way to relieve the intense discomfort was to swing both arms into the bulkhead right next to my bunk and pound the blood flow back into my swollen arms. After a half-dozen swings against the wall, my feeling would return, and I'd pass out in relief only to wake up forty-five minutes later and repeat the process. This went on every day during the short hours of sleep during the entire voyage up until the last two weeks, by then I had increased the strength in my arms and the swelling stopped.

When I returned to the deck, Justin was still out there. He looked at me with dark, swollen, glazed-over eyes and said, "Welcome to hell." At that moment, I was so sore, sick tired, hungry, cold, and miserable I actually thought I was in hell. I literally felt that if there was a hell somewhere in the universe, this was surely what it must be like.

Bringing up a full pot, *Royal Enterprise*, 1991

I felt really sorry for Justin. He was a hell of a nice kid, kind, down-to-earth, and gentle as could be. He was clearly way out of his league. As the next few days passed, he slowly began to give up the fight. He was sharped again, reducing his time off to two hours. It was obvious he was through. I was stunned at the cruelty toward someone who was clearly not built for this kind of work.

Amazingly and much to my admiration, he lasted on this impossible schedule for almost five days before he turned to me one day and said, "I just need a couple of hours' sleep, and I'll be fine."

He stopped what he was doing, walked over to Mike, and repeated to him what he had just said to me, "Mike, I just need a couple of hours' sleep, and I'll be back to work, I promise. I just need a little sleep, that's all."

He turned to walk away when Mike yelled out at him, "If you walk off this deck now, you're finished. Do you understand? There is no coming back!"

Justin stopped, turned slowly in Mike's direction, shrugged his shoulders, and in a soft voice said, "I just need a few hours' sleep." With that he turned and walked off the deck down to his cabin as was gone.

He that will not sail till all danger has
passed will never put to sea.

—Allen Villiers

Chapter 9

Jumping Ship

The sun was rising, and our work ground on. There was little time to ponder Justin's fate that day. I noticed Steve, one of the regular crew members, limping around on deck clearly in pain. I asked him what was going on.

He explained that he had been stuck in the knee by one of the long, pointed spines at the tip of a crab leg a few days ago. King crab has toxic bacteria on its shell; any cuts or puncture wound from one of the many hard spines can cause a serious infection. We all suffered from this from getting stuck through our gloves, and we were careful to treat these minor cuts immediately.

I asked if I could take a look at it. After seeing what had just happened to Justin, nobody wanted to appear to show any weakness. He told me he'd be fine and to not worry about him. Frustrated, I left him alone, shaking my head at how the mood on the ship had turned to this.

As the day progressed and the physical exhaustion of our endless work wore on us, it was becoming more evident that Steve was really struggling to keep pace with us. I finally managed to find a moment to speak with Mike about taking a look at him.

I phrased it in a way that I hoped would make sense to Mike. If I could treat his leg before it got any worse, we could possibly avoid losing Steve all together. Mike agreed but added whatever I did to treat him could not include any time off. If I could do that, then no problem. I waited until we were traveling to our next string of pots and had a half hour or so to relax.

Steve reluctantly agreed to be looked at, ever trying to appear to be a good soldier. I tried to make it as quick as possible and tried to lift his pant leg up past his knee to get a look. Steve's knee was too swollen for me to get his pants up past his knee, so time to drop his pants.

His knee had been stabbed by the long, pointed end of a crab leg. The legs of a large king crab can easily reach a foot or more in length and taper down to a very hard and very sharp, pointed spine. While sorting crab on deck and tossing the keepers over into the holding hopper, the leg spine from a large crab had punctured the skin at his knee, passing through his rain gear, sweatpants, and long underwear.

It had already swollen to the size of a golf ball, with green pus oozing from the puncture site. Without any intervention, the infection would soon completely incapacitate him. Within days he'd need to be hospitalized, forcing us to return close enough to Dutch Harbor to have him airlifted by a coast guard chopper to the airport in Dutch and flown to a hospital in Anchorage.

That was exactly why I was there, to prevent that from happening. It was difficult for me to understand the reluctance by the captain and crew to let me do my job. I understood the mind-set that had to be established to keep men toiling for endless hours in excruciating pain and discomfort. At the same time, to achieve this, common sense seemed to take a backseat.

I quickly had to come up with a plan to treat Steve's leg while he worked twenty hours a day. You have to take a moment to understand how filthy conditions on the vessel had become since we left Dutch several weeks ago. None of us had taken a shower in that time, and we'd long ago worn through any clean clothes we had brought with us by now. Working on deck and processing live king crab twenty hours a day, seven days a week has got to be one of the filthiest jobs on Earth. Being splattered with crab guts, saltwater, grease, and grime on the outside and blood, sweat, and tears on the inside quickly produced a foul mixture as the days passed, producing a ripe environment for infection to grow rapidly.

Steve had developed a raging infection. The skin was bright, flaming red for five inches around the puncture wound. When I pressed gently around the wound, green pus flowed out in large amounts. I had to move fast and aggressively if I had any chance to get this under control. As soon as Steve got off shift, I went to work.

First I literally drew a baseline around the edges of the red skin with a black marker. Then I cleaned around the puncture site and numbed the area with a few injections of lidocaine. With that done, I made a small incision in the shape of an X across the open puncture site to allow the wound to drain. Then I filled a fish tote, which is a heavy-duty plastic tub used to haul fish, or crab in our case. Big enough for a man to sit in, I would improvise and use this as a soaking tub. Filling it with warm water in a shower stall and pouring in Epsom salt to create a saltwater solution, I had him get into the tote and soak his leg in this solution.

Anyone who remembers the effects of osmosis will know how salt will draw less saline fluids to itself. In this heavy salt solution, you could actually see the pus being drawn out of the wound in a long green and red string. At the same time, I would soak his leg every day like this. I started him first on an IV drip of antibiotics his first day and then started him on oral antibiotics that he would take every six hours for ten days. Also it was critical to keep the puncture site as clean as possible and change his dressing twice a shift.

To monitor how successful this treatment was, I would examine the black marker that showed me the edge of the red inflammation area. If it continued to grow past the first mark after several days, then I had been unsuccessful in my attempt. If it began to recede back from the original mark, then the treatment was working.

Continuing on with our grueling work pace, I continued the daily treatment and could only hope what I was doing would be enough. After about forty-eight hours, it was clear that the inflammation was retreating, and the swelling was going down. Less and less fluid was able to be drawn out of the wound during the daily soaks in the Epsom salt bath. Steve was soon out of the woods, and his leg healed without any further problems. More importantly, I had managed to keep him working the entire time, thereby reestablishing my credibility with the captain and crew.

All this time, Justin had been locked in his room and not allowed to come out upon threat of violence. I witnessed an incident where some of the crew filled a garbage bag full of rotting crab guts which is one of the most putrid and disgusting things on earth and opened Justin's door to his room and flung the bag of guts onto his bed, making sure the contents of the bag spilled out onto his sheets. They then quickly closed and locked the door with Justin inside. That really hurt me to see such a malicious level of outright torment.

Meanwhile topside, the captain decided to pick up two strings of pots, about sixty, and take them to another part of the Sea of Okhotsk to see how well we'd do there. We had picked up and unloaded and dropped all the others and now were speeding about one hundred miles southeast to drop these strings and get back to our original fishing grounds.

During the operations to bring up the sixty pots and get them stowed on board, I was up on the second deck with Mike, helping him coil in the long lines of rope that connected the pots together in the string. Mike was operating a capstan, a cylinder-shaped rotating drum where a rope would be looped around. As the capstan turned, it pulled in the rope that had the pots connected to them. As the pots came out of the water, they were attached to the ship's crane and set standing on end in rows on the stern deck.

I was coiling the rope as it came up on the upper deck. At one point, the capstan froze and stopped turning. The whole process began to back up on itself, and Mike was getting really excited, shouting down for everyone to stop what they were doing before the whole deck was a tangled mess of rope and piled-up eight-hundred-pound pots. The noise was so loud from all the machinery that no one could hear him, and Mike began to panic.

He was looking frantically for his portable radio as he flipped the switch on and off on the capstan, the whole while cursing at the top of his lungs. Finally in desperation, he turned to me and yelled, "Doc, go down to the tool shack and grab a 5/8-inch crescent wrench, *now*!"

I immediately turned and flung myself down the vertical ladder that put me on the main deck. From there, I ran twenty feet to the tool locker and grabbed the thirty-pound toolbox, opened it, and rummaged through the tools until I found the crescent wrench I came for. I turned, and just as I was leaving the tool shack, I stopped in my tracks; a thought came to my mind that said to go back and get the tool box and bring the whole damn thing. Chances were Mike would end up needing something more than just this one wrench.

I quickly scooped up the toolbox and ran back to the ladder where I used one hand to hold the box and the other to pull myself up the ladder. I reached the second deck and set the toolbox down at Mike's feet.

He looked at me like, what the hell. "I said just the wrench, goddamnit, Doc."

With no time to argue, he flung open the toolbox, grabbed the wrench, and started to take off the bolts that held the outer casing on the drum. They were frozen on due to salt corrosion and wouldn't budge. Seeing what was happening, I grabbed a large hammer out of the toolbox, stepped over to Mike, and handed him the hammer; he immediately figured out what I was implying, and he began to pound loose the bolts.

By the time we had fixed the capstan and freed it back up to where it would turn again, we had needed a half-dozen different tools. Within a few minutes, we had it turning again and were back in business without a moment to spare. I thought Mike was going to bear-hug me; he was so happy that I had brought the entire toolbox. I had saved his ass, and he knew it. His huge smile lasted for quite a while after that.

That night we had the only opportunity in weeks to get a full night's sleep as it would take an estimated twelve hours to reach the drop point. Totally in a deep, sound sleep, I was shaken awake in the middle of the night by Mike.

"Doc, get up. I need your help on deck. There's a storm, and the pots haven't been tied together, and they're crashing into everything topside. Hurry up and get dressed."

"What the hell are you waking me up for?" I replied, absolutely pissed off to be so rudely brought back to my misery after such a wonderful state of blissful sleep. "I'm just a medic, goddamnit, Mike. Go wake up one of your deckhands."

"I want you up there with me, Doc. You're smart. It's as dangerous as hell out there tonight. Someone might get killed if I get one of those dumbasses out there with me. Come on, get geared up now, and follow me."

I couldn't believe it. It was the only time I was so angry for being called smart. The only night I could sleep and I, the least experienced of all the crew members, had to spend it on deck in the middle of a raging gale, dodging eight-hundred-pound crab pots as they slid back and forth across the deck and smashed into the railing.

I'll never forget the sight as I stepped out on the open deck that night. A huge full moon in a sky filled with a billion stars was coming up over the far horizon, facing the hatch I was coming out of. I was shocked to see that a furious storm was raging, with huge waves having their tops blown off by 60 mph winds. The air was filled with the white spray and mist from the tops of hundreds of white-capped waves being blown away by the howling gale; it was and still is one of the most beautiful sights I've ever seen.

The next sight was the pots slamming into the railing with tremendous force, actually bending the heavy-gauge steel in places as they hit. The pots were all sliding back and forth, standing upright on their sides as the ship listed from side to side, but at different rates of speed. So there would be spaces between them as one went one way and the other was going the other way or just a few seconds behind the one next to it.

With hands full of three-foot ropes, we began the death-defying job of tying them first to the rail then to each other one at a time, taking two steps, stopping as an eight-hundred-pound steel pot passed by, quickly taking another three steps and jumping back one as another one passed by the other way. Being hit by one was almost sure death or very serious injury, and we weren't close to a hospital.

Going from a dead sleep to dancing with death within a few minutes, I was in constant disbelief that I was out there doing this and not someone else. Slowly as we began to get more and more of the pots tied together, the level of danger diminished. After three harrowing hours in a screaming gale, escaping death by inches a hundred times, we were finished. This was an experience I'd never forget. At the time it was happening, I knew I'd never forget it. The night sky along with the howling tempest was so beautiful and the danger so intense it could never be forgotten.

Needless to say, after what had happened the day before and that night, I had become Mike's new best friend. As I made my way down to my bunk freezing cold and exhausted, I wasn't convinced this was a good thing. I collapsed in my bunk and instantly fell sound asleep.

Two hours later, it was time to resume our twenty and four shifts; all I could do was shake my head and carry on.

In the meantime, Justin's plight had grown worse. He already had to sneak to the galley without being discovered by any of the crew just to grab something to eat. Of course, I thought this was insane and did whatever I could to help him without being discovered, or I'd be in the same situation as him.

We still were scheduled to be out there for another month. I couldn't imagine this going on all that time, but there was nothing I could do about it. Every time I was relieved from my shift and was lying in my bunk, I thought of every possible excuse I could to be able to get some time off or get off the boat altogether and still get paid for the time I had put in, but I couldn't come up with any ideas. It became clear it was time to dig deep and find the will to carry on. There simply was no other option. Each day took every ounce of willpower and strength to get through. Every minute seemed like an hour, every hour a day. I had never been more miserable and in so much pain and never believed it possible for a man to endure such hardship.

Yet to my growing surprise, I somehow made it through one day and then the next. Finally we had filled our freezer to capacity of five thousand cases of king crab, which was approximately half our quota. It was time to head for the island of Paramushir, one of the northernmost of the Kuril Islands just south of the Kamchatka Peninsula.

There we'd meet up with a Japanese freighter that would take our catch to the Asian markets. We were less than a day away from there and spent our time doing some much-needed cleaning especially in the processing area. There is nothing worse than the stench of rotting crab guts, and all the slime that covered everything was already turning green.

Although we had a short reprieve from the grinding marathon we'd been subject to, there was little relief from my misery as I struggled to keep down what little food I could eat. My head spun with intense nausea as I scrubbed and chiseled the putrid remains of our last month's crabbing operations off the equipment and fire-hosed the area clean again. Several times, as the ship lurched from one side to the other and I fought to keep my balance while we listed and pitched in the autumn seas, I completely lost it. Quickly emptying the small condense from my stomach, I continued to dry heave and wrench my guts out. My stomach muscles began to cramp up, and each uncontrollable spasm brought agonizing pain along with the intense desire for death to mercifully relieve me from the torture I had found myself in.

I managed to find irony in the way God worked his plan. I had witnessed people dying when they least expected it or wished for it, and there I was, begging for death—and nothing. After one of the worst days in my life, we finally pulled into the harbor at Severo-Kurilsk on Paramushir Island. This island is made up of nearly a dozen active volcanoes, and the town of Severo was completely destroyed by a tidal wave in 1952 from one of the many earthquakes that rock this area every year.

Severo looked like a scene out of an old movie. Horse-drawn carts and 1940 vintage cars mingled on dirt streets as people dressed in traditional eighteenth-century Russian clothes went about their business. The island of Paramushir was isolated backwater as the twentieth century had passed close by but had hardly touched it. For us on deck looking out at the town, it seemed as if we had been transported back in time a hundred years.

We dropped anchor in the harbor, and immediately the Japanese freighter that had been waiting for us tied up on our starboard side. An hour later, the supply ship, the *Seattle Surveyor*, tied up on our port side. As the crew and I were handling the mooring lines, I happened to see something that I caught out of the corner of my eye, which caused me to turn and look at what was going on.

To my utter amazement, I watched as Justin with his seabag in hand made a mad dash across the deck of the *Enterprise*; and when he got near the port rail where the *Seattle Surveyor* was tied up next to us, he jumped from the deck of the *Royal Enterprise* to the deck of the *Seattle Surveyor* in one mighty leap.

Just as he did so, a half dozen of the crew on our boat who had been chasing him reached the rail and began to shout insults and threats while a couple hurled their soda cans after him onto the deck of the other ship. Justin crumpled onto the deck as he landed, made a half roll, picked himself up, and ran to the wheelhouse of the *Seattle Surveyor*.

Klyuchevskaya Volcano, Kamchatka

I stood motionless, too dumbfounded to move and not quite knowing what to do at the sight I had just witnessed. Slowly a smile grew on my face as I realized that old Justin had just pulled a fast one on these guys. Our crew was extremely pissed off and demanded that the captain of the *Surveyor* give Justin back. There was a rumor for a few hours that indeed, that was what was going to happen, and the crew of the *Royal Enterprise* delighted in what they were going to do to Justin when he was brought back. I was scared for him and couldn't believe the captain of the *Surveyor* would do such a thing. As it turned out, Justin stayed on the *Seattle Surveyor*, and a month later he returned to Seattle.

I envied him. That son of a gun had done it. He had escaped his tormentors in a seemingly hopeless situation in one of the most remote places on Earth. He saw his opportunity and did what he had to do without hesitation; my hat was off to him.

As for me, I was only halfway through this voyage. The off-loading of the five thousand cases of frozen king crab started immediately after the freighter tied up next to us. None of us slept or took more than a fifteen-minute break to find something to eat for the next twenty-seven hours. Most of the work and the hours of excruciating heavy lifting (remember each case of crab weighed ninety-five to one hundred pounds) took place either in our freezer or in the freezer on the *Kiro Maru*, the freighter we were transferring our catch to. These freezers were kept at a temperature of around twenty to twenty-five below zero, which added greatly to our misery during the torturous off-loading operation.

The motivation that kept all of us going was the simple reality that the sooner we got the job finished, the sooner this nightmare would be over. The large pallets were stacked seven levels high. The cases of crab on the sixth and seventh levels were six and seven feet high. Just lifting the heavy cases up and stacking them that high was brutal. The pace of the operations was set as fast as we could manage to keep up working as fast and as hard as humanly possible. My mind was in constant rebellion at the insane expectation that this overwhelming level of work could be accomplished.

I had no choice. I was forced to move so fast. Trying to keep up, there was nothing I could do to change anything. When you're forced to do something you think is impossible, you find yourself mentally reaching down deep into a previously unknown reservoir that is at the core of who you are as a human being. Once there, you make the choice to either pull out the strength you need to succeed or you don't. The decisions you make at moments like this define your character. Whatever choice you make has the effect of fundamentally changing you forever; it's impossible to avoid when challenged to this degree and intensity.

I found myself continually reaching down to my core to find the strength I needed to make it through those grueling twenty-seven hours. At the time, it can go unnoticed, but looking back, it was clear I changed as a man in those freezers on that tiny island in the middle of nowhere.

As soon as the last pallet of frozen crab was lifted off the deck of the *Royal Enterprise*, we prepared to get underway and return to the crabbing grounds in the Sea of Okhotsk. Only after we were well on our return trip were we allowed to get a few hours' sleep before we started the daily grind of catching and processing crab once again. I had never and have never since been more delirious with exhaustion and in such excruciating pain. I fell immediately unconscious when my head touch the heavenly cloud that was my pillow.

All of us knew that as soon as we filled the freezer hold this time, we'd be finished with this quota and be able to return to the United States. Without anyone saying anything, we all began to put a little extra effort in to our task, and the pace of our work began to noticeably increase. I noticed that I was able to actually start to put an effort into my work, whereas before I was just able to maintain the minimum amount of effort to get through the day. Now I was able to push myself to the next level which at first was a bit of a shock to me as I had come to believe I wasn't able to give any more than I had been. Soon I was delighted at my newfound strength and stamina and began to jump in to help out wherever I could.

For six weeks, we never stopped operations for anything. Each man was relieved to get something to eat or get some sleep individually throughout the day as work continued without letup around the clock. One day, in the early afternoon as we were working to bring pots up on deck and get them positioned on the launcher, the captain came over the ship's PA system and made some kind of announcement; but I could not pick out what he said due to the noise and the wind on deck. I assumed he was giving Mike some kind of instruction, so I paid little attention to it. I was in a complete daze and in a robotic frame of mind as I had been awake for days with only a few hours of scattered sleep in between.

I had found my rhythm and was focused on the work in front of me when I noticed that everyone stopped what they were doing, and one by one began to leave the deck and go in the gear room. It became less noisy as some of the hydraulics that operated the crane and the launcher were turned off. I stood motionless in the cold rain, not knowing what was going on. I hadn't heard anyone tell me to stop working, so I stood by my station wondering what was going on.

At that moment, Tim stepped up to me, his face inches from mine and screaming at the top of his lungs. He yelled in my face, "*Hey, dumbass, what the hell is your problem? We're taking a break. Get off the goddamn deck*!"

Tim was eighteen years old, about six feet tall, and weighed about 120 pounds. Because his father owned Arctic Ice Sea Foods, he had no fear or good sense when it came to his obnoxious and completely irritating behavior.

Something inside of me snapped at the belittling and disrespectful chiding I had just experienced. And I grabbed Tim by the collar of his rain gear, pushed him up against the bulkhead, lifted him an inch or two off the ground, and screamed back in his face, "*Don't you ever speak to me like that again. Do you understand me? You goddamn punk*!" And I let him go.

I turned to walk away, and as my back was turned, Tim stepped up and pushed me hard from behind. I fell to the deck, and without a thought or a split second passing, I was immediately back on my feet. I spun around and launched myself at Tim, my right fist connecting squarely to his face, which knocked him down on the deck on his back. I instantly jumped on him and managed to solidly connect several more blows to his face before I was lifted off him from behind by Mike's powerful arms.

I struggled to free myself from Mike's grasp and renew my assault on Tim who was lying on the deck, blood pouring out of his nose. Mike held on tight and began to talk me down out of my rage. "That's enough, Doc. Take it easy now." I slowly began to calm down as several members of the crew helped Tim to his feet and led him past me to the galley.

Mike let me go and told me to follow him up to the wheelhouse to see the captain. The company policy for fighting was that regardless who started the fight, both people involved will be fired, no questions asked. I knew that Tim would not be fired, so when we entered the wheelhouse, I was coming to terms with the realization that I had just lost my job. I was expecting to get my ass chewed out good by the captain for beating the snot out of the owner's son.

Instead, as Mike and I entered the wheelhouse, Mike broke out into a huge smile and slapped me on the back and announced to the captain that I had just kicked Tim's ass. Another huge smile appeared on Captain John's face. "No kidding? Nice work, Doc," he said.

"Ah, aren't I going to be fired?" I replied.

"Fired? Hell, Doc, if I had a medal, I'd give it to you," was his surprising reply. "You don't know how long all of us have wanted to kick that little shit's ass," he continued.

Mike jumped in. "You should have seen Doc. He was like a savage, and his fists were like a buzz saw." Both of them burst out laughing.

John looked at me and said, "Doc Savage, that has a nice ring to it. From now on, I'll call you Doc Savage."

"Yeah, that's great," I said. "What about me being fired?"

"You're not going to be fired, so relax," John replied. "We're going to all take a break and eat for the next hour while Dave fixes the hydraulic pump on the crane. After that we're going to get the freezer hold filled as soon as we can and get the hell out of here. Get some food and some rest, Doc. And nice work out there, you're doing good."

I turned and made my way down to the galley, shaking my head at the turn of events and at my luck.

From that day on, I was known as Doc Savage by the crew and was treated with the utmost respect and friendship by everyone on board, including Tim as he soon apologized and we became friends. For a week, he had a black eye and a swollen nose and took endless jokes by the rest of the crew in stride.

> Our goals always recede from us, salvation
> lies not in its attainment, but in the effort.
> Therefore full effort is full victory.
>
> —Gandhi

Chapter 10

Transformation

Royal Enterprise, Bering Sea, 1991

It was now October. The ice-cold wind blowing down off the Siberian steppes was numbing. Frozen rain and sleet stung our faces as it blew horizontally across the deck as we worked endlessly day and night to fill our freezer hold as soon as we could. The swelling in my arms that used to keep me up during my brief periods of sleep had subsided as I slowly gained strength in them.

I was now able to push harder and harder throughout the day, and Mike no longer felt like he had to stand over me screaming in my ear to work harder. I was now part of the crew; I knew what had to be done and was able to take the initiative without being told. All of us could feel the growing excitement that with each full pot coming on board, we were that much closer to going home.

In Alaska, the crab stocks had taken a sharp downturn in the late 80s due to the efficient and relentless crabbing operations in the Bering Sea over the last several decades. This was not the case in the Sea of Okhotsk, and our pots were filled with several hundred crabs per pot. In the Bering Sea, bringing up thirty or fifty keepers was considered a good haul. As each full pot broke the surface, cries of joy erupted from the crew, and our strength was renewed.

One day while working on deck, Tim leaned over and said, "Doc, just think, soon we'll be able to have a hot Double Whopper from Burger King. Man, that sounds good." I'll never forget how at that moment the image of a Double Whopper was the most beautiful thing I'd ever seen. The thought of how long we'd been gone and how much I loved my country swelled in my chest; funny how a hamburger could do that.

The last few weeks, the seas had turned rough and agitated by the Arctic wind. Freezing spray showered us as the *Royal Enterprise* plowed through the mounting seas. It became more difficult to concentrate solely on our work on deck as the waves began to break over the rail more frequently.

One day the waves were reaching fifteen feet high as they crashed into the side of the ship and hurled themselves over the rail. These could easily sweep a man to his death overboard. Shouts began to ring out, warning us of the impending waves' approach, whereby we'd all grab on to whatever we could and hold on for our lives as the tons of water did its best to carry us to a watery grave.

I was working the levers that controlled pulling the pots from the ocean floor. They were located right on the rail; and I needed to lean over the railing and look down into the sea to watch as the pots came into view, being careful not to let the pot hit the bottom of the boat, which would cause the line to snap and the pot to sink back down to the bottom of the ocean. Losing a crab pot filled with hundreds of king crab was worth thousands of dollars, so the pressure was real, and my concentration was completely on the water where the pot was to come into view. Jim, one of the other deckhands, was standing next to me with his back turned, coiling rope when the wave hit us.

No one had seen it coming, and all of us on deck were completely engulfed under six feet of water and swept across the deck into the bulkhead fifteen feet away. My head hit the metal bulkhead, knocking me momentarily senseless. As quickly as the wave had appeared, the water washed off the deck and was gone, leaving all of us to recover and scramble back to our feet and return to our work. Everyone was able to return quickly to their task except Jim and myself.

Mike lifted me up by the back of my raincoat collar and asked me how I was. I rubbed the back of my head and told him I'd had my bell rung on that one, but I'd be all right. "Always keep one eye on the sea and one on your work," he advised as he set my feet down on the deck.

Jim was bent over, holding his arm to his chest, obviously in pain. Mike shouted for me to look after Jim in the gear room and to get off deck before another wave swept over us again. "When you're finished with Jim, both of you get your asses back out here. We need you," Mike yelled over the sound of the wind.

Jim and I quickly made our way into the safety of the gear room and shut the watertight door behind us. "What's wrong, Jim? Are you all right?" I asked as we both slumped down onto the changing bench, relieved to finally be sitting and out of the freezing weather for the first time in sixteen hours.

"It's my hand," he explained. "I think I broke my fingers," he said, wincing in pain as he carefully tried to remove his gloves. I noticed his middle fingers were contorted into strange shapes as he realized he couldn't get his gloves off with them, angled in the way they were.

"Hold on a minute, Jim. Let me get my trauma bag, and I'll get your gloves off and take care of your hand. I'll be right back," I said. I stumbled through the narrow hallway to where my bag was and made my way back, all the while doing my best to keep my balance as the winter seas battered the *Enterprise*.

I took out my trauma scissors and cut off his rubber gloves, carefully cutting around the damaged fingers and freeing them from confines of his rain gear. We both got our first look at his fingers which were obviously fractured. The three middle ones on his right hand were bent at different angles, from ninety to forty-five degrees in the same direction. Jim held his hand up in front of his face, slowly turning his hand, trying to make sense of the bizarre sight of his fingers.

"OK, Jim, this is going to be pretty easy to fix." I began to explain to him what I was going to do. I'd experienced my fingers and my thumb being broken in high school playing football, so I knew what to do. Back then I had set my own fingers straight without any pain-blocking medication and continued to play the rest of the game, so I knew Jim would be back on deck as soon as I straightened out his fingers and splinted them together.

I told him to grasp one finger at a time and straighten and pull hard on it at the same time until it was straightened out. "I had done it in high school, so you can do it now. Strangely it doesn't hurt as much as one might think. The pain sets in later after the swelling starts."

Slowly, one at a time, Jim straightened out each finger. I had him take 800 mg of ibuprofen and used wooded splints to support and keep his fingers straight and then taped them all together for mutual support. I improvised cutting out the middle fingers of a pair of spare gloves and cutting a large square out of the other. I wrapped the rubber square around Tim's three middle fingers that protruded out of his right-hand glove and used electrical tape to join it to the rest of his glove.

I expected the ice-cold seawater and air to keep his hand on ice as we were always fighting to keep our fingers from freezing. This would, along with the ibuprofen, keep the swelling down. We geared up and opened to hatch to return to the main deck just in time to be drenched as another wave broke over the side of the ship, almost sweeping us off our feet. We quickly regained our footing and returned to our positions on the rail to continue on with our endless work and fight against the sea.

News spread that the brother of Dave, the engineer, had died in a motorcycle accident back in Ohio. Over the PA system, Captain John wanted to see a show of hands on who was in favor of finishing up our last strings of pots by all of us working straight through. He figured we could be finished in four days with all of us on deck the whole time. In this way, Dave might be able to make it back in time for his brother's funeral, which would be delayed to allow time for him to return if we got back to Dutch as soon as possible. "All in favor, raise your hands."

I was still figuring if it was humanly possible to work this hard for four days and nights straight when I noticed everyone holding their hands in the air and looking at me with *the* look. I quickly raised my hand although I was convinced this was impossible.

A sense of electricity passed through each of us as we realized we were almost finished. The way home now was pushing through everything our minds were resisting—days and nights with no sleep, little food, excruciating pain, and numbing cold. Pushing all that to the back of our minds, we began our last marathon as another pot slid off the launcher, and back to work we went.

We were by then a well-coordinated team, each of us knowing what the other could do and trusting each other with our lives as the dangerous dance with death continued. There was no holding back now, and everyone was giving their 110-percent effort. Quietly in the back of my mind, I wondered how long I could keep up this pace before I collapsed from sheer exhaustion.

The nights were the hardest time especially the early morning hours, around two o'clock on until daybreak. In the darkness of the early morning, all of us were barely able to remain standing and at every opportunity found something to lean against to hold ourselves up. One particularly difficult morning, Mike noticed me struggling to keep from collapsing. I was delirious with exhaustion when he stepped over to me and said, "When the sun comes up, you'll get your second wind, Doc. Just hold on until the sun comes up, and you'll make it."

"Until the sun comes up" became my mantra I mumbled to myself as the hours passed. Soon the outline of the horizon began to materialize as the blessed sun began its return to this side of the world. Damn if Mike wasn't right again. When the sun finally broke over the horizon, I could actually feel the surge of renewed energy and strength return. I had never experienced the profound effects that distant star could have on a person until that day. I have never forgotten that morning and how calmly and confident that old sailor Mike had spoken his encouragement to me.

Each day and night passed, blending into one another as we continued on without letup. Instead of losing strength, I could actually feel myself getting stronger and increasing my physical output as the days passed. I was really in awe of the physical body and the mind that controlled it; what a miracle of engineering. I don't know if the mind is hardwired to think there is a Creator to all life, but I admit, I found myself wondering there had to be some kind of intelligence behind such marvels I had witnessed including my own transformation on this voyage. I had several times now exceeded my own self-imposed limitations and left them far behind, dissipating in the wake of our journey.

Finally the day came when we began to pull our last string and then our last pot and then process our last case of crab. I was able to remove the headphones and earplugs that had now become part of me as the pumps and engines that ran all the equipment were turned off and fell silent. Word came of a crew meeting in the galley in five minutes; I stepped out of the processing compartment on to the open deck, greeted by a rare calm afternoon with a bright early winter sun.

It was hard to believe we were finished. A rush of mixed emotions flooded my mind as it slowly began to sink in that I had made it to the end feeling so strong. I took in a deep breath of frigid Siberian air and closed my eyes for a moment, feeling the wind blowing across my face. A deep sense of satisfaction and peace came over me. I turned away from the railing and made my way to the galley.

In the galley, we were told we were going to have twenty-four hours off starting that moment. After that we'd start twelve-hour shifts cleaning all the equipment and gear on our return trip to Dutch Harbor. A spontaneous cheer erupted from all of us gathered in the galley at the news, and immediately decks of cards were produced out of nowhere, and someone slipped a movie into the VCR and turned up the sound. You'd think after being awake for the past fifty-six hours that we'd all fall instantly into a deep sleep, but this was not the case.

I felt a strange buzz that energized me and the feeling of wanting to savor the sweet victory of our success before going to sleep. I stayed awake for several hours talking and laughing and watching parts of the movie that was playing before the buzz began to wear off. One by one, the crew began to retire to their bunks and sweet, sweet oblivion.

I awoke as if from a deep coma, not knowing right away where I was. I could feel the ship rolling gently from side to side and was brought back to my reality on board a tiny ship in a seemingly endless sea. I had been awakened for my shifts for the past two months and had no watch or clock with me, so I had no idea how long I'd been asleep or what time of day it was. I had finally staggered down to my bunk to go to sleep the day before, around five in the afternoon when the early winter sun was setting on the eastern horizon. There were no portholes in my room, and I was feeling anxious to find out the time of day to get myself to work again. I wasn't used to leisure time and felt like I might be late for my next shift, so I quickly got dressed and made my way to the wheelhouse to find out what was going on.

John was at the helm as usual, and there was a beautiful sunrise taking place outside as the backdrop to the cobalt blue windswept sea. I rubbed my eyes and yawned as I stood looking at the beautiful panoramic view from the wheelhouse.

"Good morning, John," I yawned as I stretched my stiff, tired limbs.

"Morning?" John replied. "It's not morning, Doc, it's evening." I could feel my brain switching into overdrive trying to calculate the scene I was viewing and John's reply.

"Ah, what do you mean evening?" I responded back to him, suspecting some kind of joke or prank.

"It's evening, Doc. You've been asleep almost twenty-two hours. It's the end of your tomorrow. That's a sunset, not a sunrise."

I felt a strong feeling of disorientation, and my stomach felt queasy. "Sunset," I said.

"Yeah, sunset," replied John. "You needed the sleep, Doc. I was about ready to get your ass out of the rack, so you had some time to eat before your shift started," John said.

I just stood in silence for a minute contemplating the idea of sleeping twenty-one hours straight. Finally I turned to John and said, "Thanks for the time off. No doubt I needed it. I'm going to get something to eat. I'll see you later."

With that I decided to find Mike and see what was going on next. I made my way out to the haul deck and to the rail where I'd worked so hard for months. It was quiet now save the sound of the wind and the waves and the hum of the engines as we sailed north towards Petropavlovsk. As the ship gracefully cut through the swells, the sun finally slid behind the towering volcanoes on the Kamchatka Peninsula in the distance.

It was a timeless scene, one that had remained unchanged for a hundred thousand years. Yet something had changed since the first time I saw the majestic peaks of Mother Russia. It took sometime standing by the rail before it dawned on me that I was not the same person I was two months earlier in Seattle. I felt stronger and surer of myself, more grounded; I knew this adventure had made a deep impression in my life, and I wouldn't be the same man I was when I began this voyage seemingly so long ago. I also suddenly felt hungry as hell. Taking one more look at the darkening sky, I turned smiling and made my way to the galley.

What saves me is coming home.

—Anonymous

Chapter 11

Homeward Bound

In the galley, most of the crew was watching a movie or playing cards. I was told by several crew members that we were going to start on twelve-hour shifts in the morning, so we had the night off as well. We were sailing to Petropavlovsk to drop off the three Russian biology observers and would be there in the morning. They had been monitoring our operations, keeping tabs on our quota and any bycatch or other species that we might have caught during our trip, and keeping a record of our activities.

They were all college educated, in their midforties to fifties. They lived with their families in Petropavlovsk, Kamchatka. None of them had ever owned a car before or a house, and they marveled at life in America that they were seeing on the movies they had been watching. They had never seen a VCR, color TV, ketchup, salad dressing, or a microwave oven. The galley of our boat was like a king's palace to them. During our trip, they were absolutely amazed how hard and long we worked. They said we reminded them of machines, and they had never seen anyone work as hard as we had during our voyage.

They said that Russians would never work the way we had, and they wanted to know why we did so. We were able to explain to them, when Justin was still around to interpret for us, that in America, the harder you worked, the more money you made. This was a completely foreign concept to them, and they marveled at the idea.

They explained to us that in Russia, there was no incentive to work hard because you would still only make the same very small wage no matter how long you worked or productive you were. In Russia everyone tried to work as little as possible because you'd always make the same amount of pay. They lived in seven-hundred-square-foot apartments in grey cinder block buildings. They had to ration food and were often without electricity for hours or even days at a time.

When one of them asked how many of us owned our own car, all of us in the galley raised our hand. When Mike said he owned four cars and others said they owned cars, motorcycles, snow machines, PU trucks, and motor homes, they were dumbfounded. We felt sorry for these guys and told them we would load them up with goodies when we arrived at Avacha Bay in the morning.

That night a couple of the engineers turned a couple of the brine-cooking tanks that were used to cook the king crab legs we were processing into hot tubs. These tanks were stainless steel and big enough for four men to sit in. Then with water pumped in to them and heated to near a hundred degrees, we took turns soaking and relaxing in these tanks during the night while we sailed uneventfully under a star-studded Siberian sky. After soaking in the hot water for about twenty minutes, my muscles were so relaxed I felt like rubber when I got out. Even though I had just slept twenty-three hours not long ago, I had no problem falling into a deep sleep about eleven in the evening until I was awakened by Mike at six o'clock the next morning.

I was up quickly feeling a bit uneasy at being still on the boat, but at having so much time off to sleep after months of continuous toil, the break now felt awkward. I quickly made my way to the gear room to get dressed and made my way outside on deck. The now familiar peaks that surround Avacha Bay loomed on the nearby western horizon as we were already anchored just outside the entrance to Petrapovolsk. We were waiting for the strange-looking tugboat to come pick up our Russian fishery observers. I had work to do, cleaning and disassembling machinery. Below in the galley, crew members were loading up their bags with coffee, ketchup, and a Walkman with earphones for each of them, complete with several tapes of music. They were very surprised and grateful with our generosity and tried to tell us in their broken English and hand signs that they probably would not be able to keep much of what we had given them.

Of course we were shocked to hear this and wondered out loud how this could be possible. They explained that once they reached land, they would be searched and that the security police would no doubt confiscate much, if not all, of what we gave them for themselves.

We were outraged to here this but decided to load them up with as much as possible anyway, to show them we cared about them as people if we could do nothing else. Soon in the distance, the same strange craft came into view in the distance as we said our last good-byes and handshakes on the main deck. It was a cold grey, overcast day with a steady rain falling as the tug nudged its bow up against our side, and the three men made their way over to the waiting boat. We struggled to hand over their heavily packed seabags filled with the fruits of a free society and bid them farewell. The tug slowly backed off and turned toward the misty Kamchatka coast where it soon was swallowed up by a curtain of grey rain.

Excitedly the orders were given to weigh anchor and make ready for sea. A burst of activity commenced as the anchor was raised and lines stowed. A belch of black exhaust burst from the ship's stack as the engines were engaged, and the *Royal Enterprise* responded. A turbulence of water erupted from her stern as her screws dug into the seawater slowly and laboriously moving her forward at first. Then as she gained speed, the ship seemed to gain confidence as well. Her bow began to slice through the ocean, gracefully rising and falling on the swells.

Soon a wake trailed off behind us as our course was now set at due west towards Alaska. As the hours passed, the once towering snow-covered volcanoes of Kamchatka faded into the distance and finally were gone from our sight. We were back in the open Bering Sea on the final leg of our voyage. The distant, far-flung town of Unalaska was our next port of call. Although in reality Unalaska is a tiny community on the very fringes of civilization, in our mind's eye it loomed as big as New York City or San Francisco, and our excitement at seeing this tiny outpost was running high.

We again settled into our now seemingly casual routine work on twelve-hour shifts cleaning, stowing, and dismantling machinery in preparation for our return to Dutch. At night, I again found myself at the helm of the ship during my wheel-watch shifts. This was a great time to reflect on our adventures and on my life as a whole. Being alone at night, at the controls of a ship as it plows through the inky darkness in the middle of a million square miles of ocean, can cause a person to count their blessings and see clearly what is important in their life. Each hour I marked our position down on the chart as I occasionally made a minor adjustment of the rudder to keep us from drifting off course. The *Enterprise* made her way into the night.

In the early morning hours, on the third day, I awoke Captain John when we were a hundred miles out from Dutch Harbor so he could bring her into port. I went down to my bunk to get some sleep before we arrived, but too excited at our arrival, I tossed and turned most of the time away until it was time to get up for my next and possibly my last shift.

I had no idea when my time to leave was to come. It was taboo to even hint you were wondering when you might be sent home. I was told the off-loading of our hold was to be done by dock workers and that we'd all be sent home by air from Dutch. Another crew would be flown up from Seattle for the next ten-day opilio crab season that was scheduled to start in several weeks.

We docked at the Crowley pier at about six thirty in the morning. A cold, steady rain was falling mixed with snow. As soon as we were tied up securely, the ship's crane was fired up, and most of the deckhands including myself climbed the stack of pots forty feet high and started untying each one from the other so the crane could lift them off the boat to the waiting flatbed trucks that were pulling up to receive them.

We all knew the drill, and everyone found their places on the stack, and the off-loading began immediately. I pushed the thoughts of leaving to the back of my mind and focused on the eight-hundred-pound metal pots swinging inches from my head in the morning darkness. This time of year at this latitude, it wouldn't be light until nine in the morning; and "light" was a relative term as the sky was heavily overcast with thick mist, fog, and rain. The sun's light only dimly lit the day. At that time, we worked by the light of the boat's floodlights on the mast and the streetlights that lit the pier.

I had fully transformed my attitude and mind-set to one of a crab fisherman's, and the steady rhythm of working at all times of the day and night and in any weather was already part of me. The mental battles of searching for the will and strength to carry on no longer existed. I worked steadily and calmly, knowing I could continue on like this for days if need be. It felt good to have reached this place finally after so much doubt, pain, and suffering.

It must have been around eleven in the morning when a loud voice called out to me. It was Mike standing down on the main deck, waving his large arms. "Doc, get your ass down from there. You're going home."

I stood up and handed my handful of tie-down lines to Steve, who made his way over to me gingerly crossing over the pots. As I handed him the lines, we shook hands in a firm grip.

"Take care, Doc. Thanks for everything," he said.

"Same here," I replied and began my careful climb down off the rain-soaked stack of pots.

At the bottom, Mike came over and told me that my plane was leaving in forty minutes. "So don't waste any time getting your gear packed and getting back on deck."

A taxi would be there in fifteen minutes to take me to the airport. With that, he walked away yelling something to another crewman, waving his hands. I immediately made my way to my bunk and began stuffing whatever gear I had into my bag. It was hard to contain my growing sense of happiness and feeling of accomplishment that enveloped me. My hands were shaking as I grabbed my belongings out of my locker and drawers, my mind racing with a thousand different thoughts of home and the different images from the last several months at sea.

Ten minutes later, I was back on deck, careful not to look too excited. I met Mike by the gangway where he handed me my plane ticket. He looked at me with a big grin and said, "I had my doubts about you at first, Doc, but you pulled your act together. Great job out there. Any time you want to come back, just call the office in Seattle, and you'll have a place here."

"Thanks, Mike," I said, shaking his hand, struggling not to have my hand crushed in his strong grip.

"You be careful out there."

With that I made my way down the gangway to the waiting cab.

As the plane lifted off the runway, an overwhelming feeling of joy welled up inside me. Suddenly a spontaneous cheer broke out on the plane from all the men from different boats who were on their way home. I had to laugh, realizing I wasn't the one feeling the way I was.

And it doesn't matter how many times you venture out to sea, when you're finally safe and really going home there's nothing like a good, loud, and heartfelt cheer to show your thanks for being spared this time round. I guess what saves us all is coming home.

I must go down to the sea again, the lonely sea and sky. And all I ask is a tall ship and a star to steer her by.

—John Mansfield

Chapter 12

The End or the Beginning

Landing at the airport in Seattle, having just survived my journey from the Sea of Okhotsk, I knew without a doubt I'd never return to sea again. As I hugged my roommates, Lisa and Laura, in the terminal, they recoiled in disgust at my nauseating smell. "Oh my God, you stink!" they said as each one stepped back from their embrace.

"Thanks, it's good to see you too!" I replied, somewhat surprised they didn't understand where I had been the last two months.

"We don't mean it like that. It's great to see you. It's just, well, you stink, that's all."

"Sorry, I've been wearing these clothes for two months in conditions you can never imagine," I explained. "Let's just go home."

On the way home with all the windows open, I was in a daze. I noticed that my senses were heightened, and I was amazed to see trees and how incredibly beautiful and green they were. It was around ten thirty with the morning sunlight filtering through the trees, and the sounds of birds singing was heavenly, and for the first time I began to realize just how far away I had been on my journey.

Entering my house was like entering a cathedral for the first time as a child. I fought back the urge to cry as a soft wave of gratitude washed over me. For a rare moment, I was stripped of taking my life for granted and could see clearly how wonderful it was to have a home. I went to my room, changed into some clean clothes, stuffed the clothes I had worn on the voyage into a large plastic garbage bag, and tossed them outside the back door, much to the girls' relief.

"Are you hungry?" Lisa asked. "You look like you've lost a lot of weight. You must be exhausted."

"You know, strangely I'm not hungry, and according to the bathroom scale, I've lost twenty-five pounds. I wasn't able to get any sleep on the plane. I just need to get some sleep," I answered. With that I excused myself and slipped into my own bed for the first time in a long time, catching the fleeting scent of clean sheets. I instantly fell into a deep sleep.

After a few days of R&R, I decided to buy a new four-wheel-drive truck with the money I had made on the trip. I was planning on returning to Alaska to live there someday soon and buy some remote property. I'd need a good four-wheel-drive truck. Then after a couple of weeks gaining back the weight I'd lost, I felt like it was time to get back to work as a medic for the ambulance company I'd taken a leave of absence from. Soon I was back into my familiar routine, living a good life in Seattle and pursuing my career in emergency medicine.

I noticed, a few times over the weeks while back home, the fleeting desire to return to sea had gently floated through my mind. It was unnerving to me and was quite contrary to reason. I had caught myself wondering what in the world could trigger such an outlandish desire and had quickly pushed it from my mind, each time convinced that it would be the last.

One day while at home on a day off, the phone rang, and I answered. On the other end of the line was someone asking if it was me.

"Yes, this is Erick. Who am I speaking with?"

"This is so-and-so. I work for Oceantrawl Inc. Your name was referred to us by Maritime Health Services. We are looking for an experienced medic to go to sea with our trawlers. We'd like to set up an interview with you."

I was completely taken off guard. A moment of silence ensued, at which time the person on the other end asked if I was still there. "Ah, yeah, I'm still here," I replied.

"Well, would you come in for an interview with us? We have a vessel returning to Dutch Harbor soon."

"Absolutely not. Been there, done that. Thanks for the call." With that I hung up the phone. Still shaking my head and mumbling in disbelief, the phone rang again. I answered, "Hello, this is Erick speaking."

"Don't hang up, please. This is so-and-so with Oceantrawl. What's the problem with coming in for an interview?"

"There's no problem. Just that one trip on a crab boat is plenty for me," I answered.

"Wait, don't hang up," he responded. "This will not be on a crab boat!"

Hearing that, I hesitated hanging up. "Please just give us a chance to speak with you before you make up your mind," the voice asked.

Again a pause ensued as a battle raged in my mind: common sense against the desire for adventure and a large paycheck.

Finally, after what seemed an eternity, I struggled to get the words out of my mouth. "OK, I'll come in for an interview."

Even as I spoke the words, I was in disbelief I was actually saying them. We arranged a day and time, and with that the conversation was over. After hanging up, I was angry with myself for agreeing to such a stupid thing as even considering another voyage on the Bering Sea.

After calming down, I justified my decision by convincing myself I'd just go through the motions of the interview, knowing full well I'd never sign another contract. *Yeah, that's it. I'll just pretend to be interested, and after the interview I'll decline the offer—an excellent plan, a very smart move on my part.* I patted myself on the back for being so crafty and went on about my day without further thought on the subject.

Soon the day arrived for my interview, and I confidently arrived on time. I was ushered in the office with the personnel rep, and the interview began.

"I was told you were very hesitant to come and speak with us. Can you explain why?" she politely asked.

"Yeah, sure I can explain. Have you ever been on a crab boat on the Bering Sea?" I asked.

"No, I haven't. I have heard it is a very difficult job," she replied in a calm, understanding voice. "We don't own any crab boats in this company. We are a trawler company, which is completely different than what you experienced," she continued.

"Different in what way?" I asked, for the first time beginning to become interested in what she had to say.

"What schedule did you have on the *Enterprise*?" she asked.

"Twenty on and four off on a routine day, more if deemed necessary," I answered.

"Well, you see, you'd be on a twelve on and twelve off with us," she smiled, knowing I'd like to hear that. She continued, "You worked on deck, I presume?"

"Yes, I did," I answered.

"Well, there you are again," she said. "You will not work on deck for us. As a matter of fact, you will not go outside unless you want to get some fresh air or observe the scenery," she added.

"How is that possible?" I shot back, ignorant of the different types of fishing vessels and how they operated. This all sounded too good to be true and a setup on her part to shanghai me back out to sea.

"Because you'll be on a trawler, not a crab boat. They're completely different operations," she answered. "You'll be the ship's medic, and we'll cross-train you to work in quality control. You'll learn more about that later, but it entails taking readings off various gauges and entering data. Twelve on and twelve off, crew share on the catch that can total $14,000 a month, with a guarantee of $200 a day if the catch results in less pay than your guarantee. Sound like you might be interested now?" she asked.

I wasn't prepared to be convinced, so I was cautious with my answer. "Ah, yeah, it sounds good," I slowly answered, all the while trying to think of some good reason to get up and run out of the room and never look back.

Not missing a beat, she pushed a contract across the table in front of me.

"One of our vessels is leaving very soon. What's your decision?" she asked, looking directly into my eyes, studying my reaction. Feeling some pressure and with my mind reeling with all sorts of conflicting thoughts and emotions, I met her stare with mine; and after a few seconds, I replied, "Sure, why not?"

She handed me a pen and with the now familiar words said, "Just sign right here."

On the way home from the interview, I kicked myself in the ass for being so easily persuaded. I tried to convince myself that I'd made the right decision, but I could not. I had a feeling of dread and was filled with anxiety. In the back of my mind, I began to notice a strange and perplexing calm unaffected by the turmoil that the rational part of my mind was going through; and although in complete denial, I intuitively knew it was the call of the sea.

As I drove home, I began to relax, slowly realizing that like the thousands of men that had preceded me over the past millennia, the salt spray and wind and the eternal mystery of the sea was in my blood now. At that moment, I knew there was no use fighting it. I was hooked; I was going back to sea again; it was destiny, and I'd just have to let it run its course.

As I pulled into the driveway and turned off the truck's engine, I sat for a moment as the anxiety I had been feeling moments before evaporated, replaced by a growing sense of purpose and direction. Something my father use to say to me growing up as a child came to my mind. I had never understood what it meant until this moment. "Be careful what you ask for because you just might get it."

I wanted freedom ... open air ... and
adventure; I found the sea.

—Alain Gerbault

Chapter 13

Voyages of the Northern Jaeger
1991-1996

The *Northern Jaeger* was built in Bremerhaven, Germany, in 1989. She is 337 feet long and 51 feet at the beam, with a top speed of 14 knots (17 mph) and displaces 6,978 tons. At the time she was built, she was the Cadillac of the sea. From her catch of pollock, she could produce and burn in her engines thirteen thousand gallons of fish oil, saving Oceantrawl Inc. tens of thousands of dollars in diesel fuel each voyage. She was built to carry a crew of 110 people but routinely sailed with up to 180, made up of individuals from all over the world.

Dutch Harbor sits on the edge of a frontier where a modern-day gold rush was taking place in the 1980s and 90s. Fortunes could be made from the profits of fishing the incredibly bountiful Bering Sea. Even a regular Joe from anywhere could strike it rich—if they had what it took to venture out onto one of the last great wild places left on Earth.

The work done on these vessels is not the same kind of work done by land lovers. Like everything to do with the Bering Sea, the work done there is extreme in nature. Perhaps one in a hundred people could endure this kind of work for more than a few hours, and many who arrived to give it a go failed. Crew members on trawlers signed sixty—to ninety-day contracts. The ship had two full crews that rotated in and out every sixty to ninety days.

Factory workers worked a grueling six on and six off seven days a week the entire trip. Other members of the crew worked twelve on and twelve off 24/7. The conditions are luxurious for a fishing boat; yet nonetheless it's cold, wet, repetitious, and very painful. Working as a processor on a factory trawler is one of the most painful and miserable jobs in the world and extremely dangerous.

There are dozens of different types of machines used to behead and sort and skin the fish. All of them have blades and sticks rotating and swirling around just waiting for a mistake by an exhausted factory worker.

There were two main seasons called A and B seasons; these were targeting pollock, a little-known species outside of the Bering Sea. Pollock comprise of the largest landings of any single fish species in the United States or the world.

More than three million tons are caught each year from the Bering Sea off Alaska. Pollock are in the cod family and make up a huge biomass species that are the base species that support the ecosystems

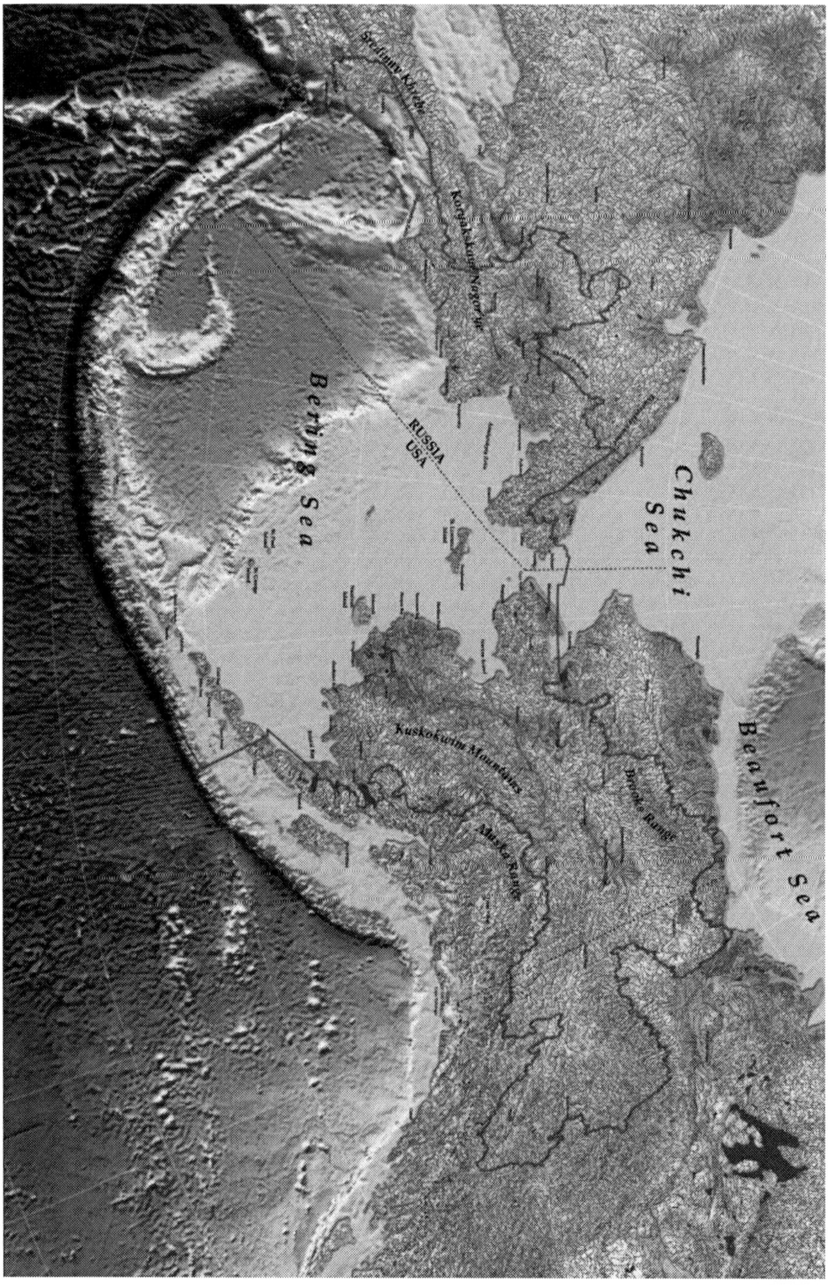

The Shallow Bering Sea

of the northern ocean off the coast of Alaska, Russia, and Japan. Alaskan pollock is the largest remaining source of palatable fish in the world. Remember those fish sticks you loved as a child? Or fish fillet sandwiches from McDonald's, Long John Silver's and a million other outlets? That's pollock.

In one day alone, when I was on board the *Northern Jaeger* in her peak years, we pulled one hundred tons of pollock over the stern to process into surimi. To me it was mind-boggling to try and comprehend the size of the schools of pollock roaming the Bering Sea. So vast are these schools that any collapse of their biomass would have devastating consequences for the world's food supply and the entire Bering Sea ecosystem. Halibut, salmon, Steller sea lions, fur seals, and whales all eat pollock. One of the reasons for this incredibly rich ecosystem is the geological makeup of the Bering Sea.

The Bering Sea is a relatively shallow sea compared to the Pacific Ocean that lies next to it. The strong currents that come off the Pacific bring nutrients from her depths up onto the Bering Sea floor, providing a rich source of food for the creatures dwelling in the Bering Sea. I knew none of this before arriving on board the *Jaeger* where a whole new world opened up to me.

The Walleye Pollock

It's in this context that a modern-day Alaskan gold rush was created. Along with the pollock fisheries, there're the crab, salmon, halibut, herring, and others. Hundreds of millions of dollars are at stake, but the biggest moneymaking product from pollock is surimi.

Before the two-hundred-mile limit became law in the 80s, pollock was primarily fished off the Alaskan coast by foreign fishing fleets from Japan and Russia. The Japanese make a paste out of pollock meat called surimi. From this they make a dozen products or more. They're willing to pay a lot of money for this product, and after the two-hundred-mile limit went into effect, their trawler fleet was excluded from fishing most of the Bering Sea.

American fishing companies scrambled to fill the void and cash in on the newly created market. So much profit was possible that contracts to build the state-of-the-art surimi trawler fleets were signed, and building began immediately in shipyards here in the United States and Europe. For Oceantrawl Inc., this included three massive trawlers: the *Northern Jaeger*, *Northern Eagle*, and the *Northern Hawk*, or the "bird boats" as they were affectionately called; all three nearly identical and all classified and geared to turn pollock into surimi.

Turning pollock into surimi is as much an art as it is a science and takes an entire deck three hundred feet long packed with state-of-the-art machinery and nearly one hundred factory workers working in shifts around the clock to pull it off. The haul deck is the main deck that is exposed to the elements and where the trawl net is set and hauled in with the catch. The second deck below the haul deck is the factory where the pollock are turned into surimi and shaped into fifty-pound blocks cased in cardboard boxes and sent to the third deck or the freezer hold. The *Northern Jaeger*'s freezer hold could hold up to sixty-five thousand cases of surimi or three thousand tons. On a good trip, we could fill the hold in fourteen days. My share alone would total $6,500.

Cross-section of a surimi trawler

I'm not going to go into too much detail about surimi production as I could write an entire book on the subject. I just want to set the scene so you get an idea of where the rest of this story takes place.

It was January 1991. I was flown to Dutch Harbor from Seattle to meet the *Northern Jaeger* when she came into port to off-load her catch and rotate out her crew for a new one to start another contract. I was nervous as hell and apprehensive about the voyage as I didn't believe a word of what I was told to expect back at the office in Seattle.

I sat passively resigned to my fate as I gazed out the window from thirty-five thousand feet, watching the world change below while the hours passed from green and inviting to grey and white and foreboding. The gently rolling countryside below filled with the warm glowing lights of small towns and cities gave way, the farther north we flew, to endless wilderness of jagged snow-covered peaks without any sign of life.

It's two thousand miles north to Anchorage from Seattle and then another eight hundred miles east across the Bering Sea to Dutch Harbor. A small twin-engine plane flew us to Dutch. Sitting in my seat, I could see into the cockpit and out the front windshield of the plane as well as out the side from the window at my seat.

Flying into Dutch Harbor is one of the more thrilling experiences one can experience especially at dusk, below the clouds at about four hundred feet over water. Weaving through fiords so narrow, the wing tips had only a hundred-foot clearance on both sides of the plane while passing through patches of fog that hung over the water. With the pucker factor set at high, I watched transfixed as the pilots threaded their way through the canyons and onto the tiny runway, slamming on the brakes with full flaps set to keep us from hurtling into the bay at the end of the ridiculously short runway.

"Welcome to the end of the world," the pilot greeted us. "Have a nice stay."

When I arrived at the pier, off-load was in full swing. I had no idea who or where to go to find someone to help me figure out what I was supposed to do. Off-load is extremely fast paced and hectic; speed is of the utmost importance. Getting the ship unloaded, resupplied, and a new crew on board as fast as possible is critical. Ships don't make money at the dock, and the money clock is always ticking.

Runway at Dutch Harbor, Alaska

I wandered around until I found the galley, looking for someone who I thought might help me. I was told a couple of names by crewmen on break of the people I should try and find.

As time passed and I wasn't doing anything, I grew increasingly stressed. On the *Royal Enterprise*, standing around doing nothing was a major sin. I didn't want to start out by having my supervisor yelling at me for standing around humping the poodle. I managed to get hold of a freezer suit that fit me and made my way down to the freezer hold.

Everything about the *Northern Jaeger* was huge compared to what I had been used to. The *Northwind* was 282 feet long, and the *Royal Enterprise* was 110; both were old veterans of the sea and had seen their best days. The *Northern Jaeger* was 337 feet long and brand-new. Everything was clean and shiny, resembling a hotel with long hallways and doors every ten feet or so.

Northern Jaeger at port, Dutch Harbor, Alaska

The freezer hold was like a cathedral, huge with the ceiling thirty feet overhead, fifty feet wide, and two hundred feet long. It was twenty-five degrees below zero. Down through an open hatch, a pallet was lowered to the deck where half a dozen men waited as clouds of water vapor streamed from their mouths and noses with each breath.

A line of men stretched out and up onto an enormous mountain of cases of frozen surimi stacked to the ceiling. As soon as the pallet hit the deck, the men started stacking cases on it as fast as possible. I found a space next to one of them and started grabbing the forty-five-pound cases and stacking them on the pallet with the others.

As I caught the eyes of those around me, I noticed they were looking at me rather strangely. At first I ignored them and continued to stack cases, quickly working up a sweat under my freezer suit despite the subzero temperatures that stung my exposed skin. Finally the foreman of the freezer crew came up to me and asked who I was.

"My name is Erick. I'm the medic on the next trip."

A huge smile swept across his face as he introduced himself. "I'm Paul, and what are you doing down here anyway?" he asked, seemingly confused by my presence.

"I'm working. What do you think I'm doing?" I was confused at such a dumb question.

"Hey, look, Doc, you're on the next voyage, not this one. You're not supposed to be down here. Go back up to the galley, and wait for me there, and I'll get you squared away on my break in about fifteen minutes. It's OK, relax. Just wait for me there."

"OK," I replied, relieved to finally have someone who knew what was going on to help me. I eagerly made my way out of the freezer hold and up to the warm confines of the galley. I found a seat at one of the tables and sipped on a glass of orange juice, waiting for Paul to show up.

When Paul showed up, he didn't waste any time and motioned for me to follow him. I grabbed my gear and followed up several fights of stairs until we were as far up in the superstructure as one could go, at "officers' country" as we'd call it in the military: the staterooms next to the wheelhouse. There were the captain's and first mate's cabins along with the first engineer's and purser's and, to my total surprise, mine. These cabins were huge staterooms, like large master bedrooms. On a ship where space was a premium, this was pure luxury.

Paul showed me in and explained to me that this voyage was not over until off-load was finished I had time to stow my gear and get something to eat. He'd let the powers that be know I was there, and I was to wait in my room for further instructions.

"Welcome aboard," he said as he left and was gone, leaving me alone in my amazement at my living quarters. For the first time, I started to reconsider my apprehension about returning to work on a fishing boat. Maybe this was going to be different than a crabber.

Over the next thirty hours we were in port, I met the captain, Tim, the first mate, Brooks, and the purser, Mac, as well as a dozen others including the factory foremen, Paul and Lorie, as well as the head of the Quality Control Department, Don. Don was in his twenties with a degree in food science. He'd be my immediate supervisor in Quality Control as I was to be trained as a QC tech. As for my medical duties, I answered to the captain. With all the formalities completed, the day came to cast off and return to the fishing grounds in the Bering Sea.

On this voyage, we had a crew of 180 people. As the *Northern Jaeger* slowly moved out of the bay at Dutch, I was aware of the fact that I was responsible for the welfare of a lot of people and felt the pressure. I spent my time inventorying the sick bay and all my medicine and medical gear in the infirmary. I was nervous as hell because I knew it was only a matter of time before I'd be confronted with my first case. Everything about this experience was new and strange.

I hated being the new guy and was anxious to get some experience and feel more confident in my duties. I'd be working twelve on and twelve off, from six in the morning to six in the evening in the QC lab located right in the middle of the processing factory on the second deck. This too was completely new to me as well, and I had no idea about what went on there. So I had a lot coming at me all at once, which was good because it kept my mind occupied and made the days fly by.

The first week, I spent my time being trained in the lab. Settling in to the daily grind, I had no complaints as this was a piece of cake compared to the *Enterprise*. Then the day came when I was off duty around eight in the evening, and an urgent knock was on my cabin door.

"Doc, one of the factory workers got his hand caught in an auger. Tore his hand up pretty bad. You better come quickly."

"I'm on my way," I replied and grabbed my trauma bag I had prepared for just such an occasion. I followed the messenger down to the factory to the extruding area.

There the pollock, already ground into paste, was put into a final mixing tub that rotated around; and preservatives consisting of sugars were poured in. A larger auger pulls the paste out of the tub and on its way through the factory. Reaching into the turning tub was common to help get all the paste out before the next batch would be poured in. It took a quick and alert hand not to get yourself caught up in the auger blades. That night the auger had won.

This was when I met Henry. He was thirty years old and was from Poland. He had escaped from the Iron Curtain when the Russian trawler he was a crew member on had made port at Seward, Alaska, back in 1988. At the first opportunity, he jumped ship and turned himself in to authorities in Anchorage. Granted asylum, he returned to what he knew best and soon found himself back at sea aboard an American trawler.

We found Henry not far from his workstation, his right hand wrapped in towels, and he was sitting patiently, waiting for me. I introduced myself and gently removed the bloody towels to get a look at his hand. The auger had made a perfect circular spiral cut starting at the tip of his index finger and traveling up the middle of his hand. At that point the machine was turned off, and he was able to extract his hand. The incision was a quarter-inch wide and down to the bone.

What struck me about Henry was his good-natured attitude even though I knew he must have been in a great deal of pain. We went to the ship's infirmary which was just an empty cabin with a couple of bunks and cabinet space to hold my medical supplies. He made himself comfortable while I prepared my suturing setup. I prepared a syringe of lidocaine to numb around his laceration. As I drew near with the syringe, he politely refused the injection. Always smiling, he let me know it wouldn't be necessary.

It was obvious to me that he didn't understand that I was going to have to sew his wound up, which would take several dozen stitches, so I began to carefully explain what I needed to do. With a smile he politely cut in, in his Polish accent, telling me he knew what I needed to do; and he did not need any lidocaine.

"You're sure?" I needed to double-check.

"I'm sure," he answered.

"OK, how about 800 mg of ibuprofen? At least that is something,"

"Not necessary" came his reply.

I was really confused by then. "Why won't you take anything for pain, Henry? What's up with that?"

"I was jailed by the Russians several times when I lived in Poland," he went on to explain, "and I was beaten very severely. The only way for me to survive was to endure the pain, learn to control it, and not give in." He said, "I'm not going to use any pain medication tonight, so just get on with what you have to do. I'll be fine."

Not convinced, I proceeded with my task with the help of Maria who spread out all of the thread and needle, forceps, and gauze pads. I took special care to clean out the wound using a soft brush and antiseptic soap. I then ran the thread and fishhook needle through a bowl of alcohol to sterilize everything as completely as I could, secondary infection being my greatest concern.

Then nervous as hell, hoping I'd remember everything I'd been taught back in Seattle, I pushed the suturing needle through the skin on one side of the laceration, starting at the tip of Henry's finger. Glancing up to see Henry's reaction, I expected him to finally give in to some lidocaine. I was met with a gentle smile and a nod signaling it was OK to continue.

I pushed the needle through the other side and stitched the thread up tight, bringing both sides of the deep cut together, tied a knot, cut the thread, and began the process over again. After every few stitches, Henry and I would look each other square in the eyes, each one of us giving the other the unspoken OK to continue on. With each push of the needle through his skin without so much as a whimper, I grew more and more impressed with his character.

Finally the last knot was tied and thread cut. He held up his hand to get a good look. It was a gnarly sight with his finger and hand already swollen twice its normal size and black stitches straining to hold the whole thing from exploding. Nevertheless he thanked me with a smile.

"If the pain gets to be too much, don't hesitate to let me know," I said as he got up to leave.

"I will, Doc, thanks again."

"I'll make arrangements to have you taken back to Dutch," I explained."

"I don't want to leave. I'll be able to work in a day or two," was his reply.

"Look, Henry, you're hurt pretty bad, you know. You'll get paid for the rest of the trip even if you're at home, right?"

"Just give me a couple of days. I will be able to return to work, I promise you," he insisted. I looked him in the eyes, studying his features, looking for any signs of second thoughts he might be having. Seeing nothing but sheer determination, I gave in.

"OK, I'll give you two days then we'll take it from there," I replied.

"Thanks, Doc," he answered and turned and left.

I turned to Maria, "That's one tough dude," I said. "One tough dude!"

We cleaned up, and I finished all the necessary paper work, satisfied with my first suturing job. I made my way to my room and retired for the night. Tomorrow was another day, and I knew there would be more to follow.

I was now like a doctor of a small town, a very remote small town. It had Mexicans, Filipinos, Japanese, Vietnamese, and Eastern Europeans, as well as Americans from every state and every walk of life. Once we left the dock, it was too late for any second thoughts about being on board. There was no going back unless the danger of the loss of life or limb presented itself.

Very quickly the toll of the relentless schedule began to separate the men from the boys. My job was to keep everyone working to the best of their ability without endangering anyone's health. As the days wore on, the weak and confused did their best to find some medical excuse to get time off from their ordeal. Daily I had someone come to me with questionable aches and pains or mysterious illness, asking for a shift or a day off. Mixed in with those were the minor cases of sprains, aches, rashes, cuts, bruises, minor infections, and the occasional dental case.

I set up my medical office during the day in the QC lab where I worked as it was located right in the middle of the factory so was easily accessible. A balance of treating legitimate cases and getting those who were faking their symptoms to get some time off back out on the line became a valuable skill. Word quickly spread to the company heads back in Seattle that they were getting their money's worth and to the crew that they would be well taken care of but that I was no pushover.

Always looming in the background as deck and factory operations ground on around the clock was the realization that a serious accident was not an if but a when. I could never completely relax knowing this and was always on edge, wondering if I'd be up to the task. I was one of the only few EMTs in the entire Bering Sea in those days, in nearly eight hundred thousand square miles of total wilderness where the most dangerous jobs in the world were performed. So I wasn't surprised when two days later while I was working in the QC lab, a factory worker burst into the lab shouting for me to come quick; one of the other QC technicians, Dan, had fallen through the deck grating and impaled himself on a level sensor rod.

"What the hell?" I grabbed my trauma bag. Once again, I followed the messenger through the maze of machines and pipes, conveyer belts, and pumps to where Dan was lying on the slimy deck grating. He was pale and covered in sweat, clearly in shock. I knew he was hurt bad and quickly started my exam to find what the damage was.

This was one of the more bizarre accidents I'd seen up until this time. The grating that was in place to walk on in the factory was raised about two feet above the metal deck. A series of metal framework was welded to allow different-shaped heavy-duty plastic grating to be fitted around all the various machines in the factory. Wastewater flowed underneath and drained into the bilges.

The grating was cut into various sizes and shapes like a puzzle, allowing for sections to be removed if work needed to be down below their level. Apparently a small section, only three by three feet, had been removed next to a water tank and left open, unattended. Dan had come along focused on reading the various gauges and stepped into the hole.

Attached to the water tank was a level sensor, a stainless steel half-inch-diameter rod with a sensor attached that could be adjusted up or down and tightened in place, allowing water to fill the tank to the desired level. Upon reaching the sensor, a pump would be turned on, draining the tank automatically. The steel rod protruded about eighteen inches above the tank's rim.

When Dan fell, he instinctively reached out his arm to catch himself. On his way down, this allowed the steel rod to impale him in his underarm, driving the rod through all of his clothes and up into his underarm, stopped only by his shoulder bone. He somehow managed to lift himself up and pull the rod out of his body before collapsing on the deck and calling for help.

That was where I found him. He was in excruciating pain and in shock, bleeding heavily from his wound. I glanced over to get a look and the diameter and length of the rod and noticed it was covered in a thick gelatinous film of yellowish fish slime. I realized I had a very serious situation on my hands; not only was he impaled at least six inches into his body, but with the rod covered in fish slime, the onset of a serious infection was of little doubt now. The consequences could be extremely serious.

Time then was of the essence. He had to be moved quickly to a clean, warm, and dry place where I could treat him. Using my trauma scissors, I cut off his raincoat and multiple layers of other clothes he was wearing from his waist up. Grabbing a thick eight-by-eight-inch trauma pad, I placed it up under his shoulder over his wound and had him hold his arm against his side to keep the dressing in place.

I assisted him up, swung his uninjured arm over my shoulder, instructed a factory worker to grab my trauma bag, and off to the infirmary we went. Moving as quickly as I could, I managed to get him up to the infirmary and into a clean bed. I then began to examine the wound. It resembled a gunshot wound, as a round, neat, and open half-inch hole.

I placed a stack of pillows on the bed and placed his legs over them. Being elevated, that helped keep his blood in his extremities flowing back into his torso, increasing his blood pressure to his vital organs. He had lost a lot of blood, so I packed the wound full of gauze strips. It was a gaping hole, and you could see all the way into it. I pushed strip after strip into the wound until it was full and then placed a thick gauze pad over it and applied direct pressure, taping it firmly into place by wrapping tape around his chest tight.

I then started a saline IV drip in his arm and took a reading of his vital signs. He was complaining about numbness radiating down his arm and painful tingling and burning sensations. This was a bad sign as there is a major nerve bundle, the auxiliary, located in the underarm area. This is one of the areas in the body where nerves running throughout the body bunch together before separating again, much like a freeway junction. It was apparent the rod had hit this nerve bundle, causing the symptoms he was experiencing.

I had treated him for shock, had his bleeding under control, and stabilized his vital signs. I needed to clean out his wound the best I could as quickly as I could. After waiting a half hour for his bleeding to stop, I carefully unwrapped the bandages and using tweezers, slowly pulled the strips of bloody gauze out of his wound. I then used a large syringe without the needle, filled it with saline solution and hydrogen peroxide, and flushed the wound. Generating pressure by pushing down on the syringe plunger, I was able to get deep into the puncture, irrigating his wound for several minutes.

Finally satisfied I had cleaned his wound the best I could, I packed the deep hole in his underarm again with sterile gauze. I left it uncovered so it could drain, and finally I gave him an oxycodone for pain and made sure he was as comfortable as possible. I was finished with him for the moment.

I went immediately to the bridge where Brooks was on duty for the night shift and let him know that we needed to make arrangements to get Dan to a hospital as soon as possible. He would see if there were any vessels near us. We could transfer Dan to one that was heading into Dutch Harbor.

It was getting late by now, and I decided I'd fill out all the paperwork in the morning. I had no idea when I'd be called on again to give medical treatment. I had learned by then to get what sleep I could whenever possible. Satisfied I had done all I could for one day, I found my way to my bed and immediately fell fast asleep.

Royal Enterprise, Sea of Okhotsk, 1991

Cemetery, Dutch Harbor, Alaska

Avacha Bay, Petropovalisk, Kamchatka

Erick Connell

Coming out of the freezer hold, thirty degrees below zero

Emptying a pot, *Royal Enterprise*, 1991

Aleutian Islands coastline, Alaska

Royal Enterprise, Sea of Okhotsk, Russia, 1991

Petropovalisk, Avacha Bay, Kamchatka, 1991

Royal Enterprise, Sea of Okhotsk, Kamchatka, 1991

Bringing up a net, *Northern Jaeger*, 1993

City of Unalaska, Dutch Harbor

Russian Orthodox Church, Dutch Harbor, Alaska

Passing a freighter near Dutch Harbor, Alaska

BEYOND THE NORTHERN HORIZON

Northern Jaeger, Bering Sea, 1992

D127E
Working on deck, *Royal Enterprise*, Sea of Okhotsk, Kamchatka, 1991

Emptying a full net of pollock, *Northern Jaeger*

D128E
Setting the net, *Northern Jaeger*, 1993

On deck the *Northern Jaeger*, Bering Sea, 1993

On deck, *Royal Enterprise*, Sea of Okhotsk, Kamchatka

I awoke suddenly, sitting up in my bunk and quickly looking over at my clock—five in the morning. I had left instructions with the night foreman to keep an eye on Dan and if they thought I was needed, to wake me right away. I quickly got dressed and made my way to where he was and checked in on him.

He was awake, doing fine. I decided to change his dressing. Using forceps and tweezers, I gently pulled the strips of old gauze out of his gaping wound one at a time, looking intently for any signs of infection.

After the last one was out, I used a small flashlight to peer down into the six-inch-deep hole in his flesh, checking on the condition of the tissue. Everything looked good so far, much to my relief. I then repacked his wound with clean sterile gauze, made sure he got some breakfast, and then made my way to the wheelhouse to see what luck Brooks had locating an inbound vessel.

Again I was relieved to hear he had been able to contact the trawler *Dynasty*. She was en route as we spoke and would be there in a few hours. The weather was holding just at the edge of what was considered safe to launch a Zodiac inflatable boat. It looked to me like it was going to be a hairy ride in a boat so small as the seas were large and menacing, yet I was grateful everyone was taking Dan's injury seriously.

I went down and arranged for Dan's bag to be packed and wrote out a set of instructions for the captain of the *Dynasty* to follow in caring for Dan while on board. I also checked with Henry to see if he really could go back to work or if he needed to go as well. He demonstrated how, if he had to, he could work with one hand and that he wasn't leaving unless I'd carry him to the Zodiac. With that, how could I make him leave? Only Dan would be transferred.

Ships dare not get within a quarter-mile to each other in those treacherous waters. The wind, currents, and waves can easily bring two ships on a collision course before there was time to react. As the *Dynasty* finally approached us, she kept a respectful distance as preparations were made to launch the Zodiac. As the boat crew and

Dan climbed into the small boat, a sense of excitement permeated the air. This was going to be a wild ride.

You don't really get a perspective on just how powerful and big the waves are until you see a tiny Zodiac, with four men in it, hovering over the massive swells. The waves go from lapping at the bottom of the small boat to being twenty feet below it, boiling in foam and spray within seconds. One gets the sense that the sea was daring us to release the tiny craft into its clutches. Timing was everything as everyone braced for the moment of release. As the sea rose up to within inches of the bottom of the zodiac's hull, the line was released.

Like a roller coaster on liquid rails, the Zodiac was on its way. First down into a deep valley between waves, where we lost sight of it, then up the other side; all the while its tiny but powerful motor was zipping the amazingly agile craft over the water at an astonishing speed. Within moments, it had covered the distance between the trawlers and was raised up the side of the hull of the *Dynasty*.

A few minutes later, after Dan was helped out of the Zodiac, the delicate ballet with death resumed as the process of lowering the boat and returning took place without incident. I was impressed at the skill and courage of the two crews and as silly as it may sound, at the generosity of the Bering Sea for allowing us to complete the task safely.

I know I'm not the first sailor to feel that the sea is alive and has a soul of its own. There's simply too much power and beauty to escape having thoughts like these. At moments like this, one feels a connection to one's ancestors. For even with all of today's technology, the steel, electricity, and size of modern ships, the oceans can make a man feel very, very small and helpless and even hopeless at times.

Weeks passed on my first voyage with the *Jaeger*. Slowly my "I'm the new guy" anxiety began to recede as I had successfully treated several serious injuries and was dealing with the steady stream of minor cuts, sprains, and tendonitis with a growing reputation as being attentive and fair in my treatment.

The day finally arrived when our massive freezer hold was stuffed as full as we could get it, and it was time to return to Dutch Harbor.

As the last of the pollock made their way through the factory, being turned into surimi and packed in cases and finally made their way to the freezer, the factory fell silent; and the labor-intensive task of cleaning began. One thing became clear to me. Work, a lot of hard work, never stops on a trawler. Every square inch of the factory and its entire jumble of machinery had to be meticulously cleaned and sterilized. Everything had to be taken apart, with hundreds of parts scrubbed, powerwashed, and sanitized. This was a miserable task that had to be done often and one everyone cursed. By the time this was accomplished, the vessel was arriving in Dutch and it was where the real work began, the dreaded off-load.

On the *Royal Enterprise*, we had five thousand one-hundred-pound cases in a minus-thirty-degree hold. Everyone worked straight through until all cases had been transferred over to the freighter. It had taken us thirty-six hours nonstop.

On the *Northern Jaeger*, we had sixty-five thousand forty-five-pound cases and around a hundred people working in shifts to accomplish this. It all was the same in the end—the hardest, most miserable work anyone would ever do.

As for me, I could hardly contain my joy when it was explained to me that as a QC tech, my job during off-load was to be up on deck taking inventory as the pallets, stacked with cases of surimi, were lifted out of the freezer hold and over to the Japanese freighter. All I needed was warm clothes and a pen and paper. I could not believe my good fortune. This really was different than a crab boat.

The thought came to me that I could actually do this for a living. With the freezer filled in only three weeks, my share was $6,500. We still had enough time in the sixty-day contract to do this at least one more time if not twice before I was finished with this trip and went home; $20,000 in two months' time wasn't bad. I realized then that this was what I was going to do from then on. This was my life already. I shook my head slowly in disbelief. Who would have thought a month ago I'd be making my living sailing the Bering Sea?

Life is either a great adventure or nothing.
—Helen Keller

Chapter 14

Return to Kamchatka

I returned to Seattle after seventy-four days at sea, and although I had it relatively easy, being at sea for any length of time takes a lot out of a person. I was going to sail again with the *Northern Jaeger* from Seattle to Dutch Harbor in a couple of months, but for the meantime, I was home. What a great feeling it was to be back.

I had a great feeling of accomplishment as well as a tremendous feeling of gratitude for all the small things most people take for granted. Trees, grass, friends, family, and comfort all took on a new meaning, bringing me a level of happiness I had not often experienced before going to sea.

After several weeks off, enjoying the fruits of my labor, I decided to return to work on an ambulance again. I did not need the money as my pay for working on an ambulance was a fraction of what I made at sea; it wasn't the money. I could do the work as a medic comfortably as long as I felt I was trained to the highest level I could be. I liked being confident working as a medic on a ship in the Bering Sea or on an ambulance in a major city. If you're not sure you know what you're doing, you shouldn't be there. The only way to be able to meet the mental challenge that emergency medicine required was to do it; it could not be acquired by reading a book. I kept this schedule of working on the ambulance between trips as the year passed, and my experience and expertise grew. During one of the two months I had off, I traveled to New Zealand and Australia and visited my best friend on Maui on my return flight.

The year passed with me gaining more and more experience and confidence with each voyage. It was already December 1992 when the day came to take leave of my job in Seattle and return once again to my job on the *Northern Jaeger*. I was ready and felt sharp and on top of my game. I could swear I could feel a little saltwater flowing in my veins.

When I went to the office to sign my contract, I was informed this one would be for ninety days as Oceantrawl Inc. had negotiated a contract with the new Russian government to fish for pollock off the coast of Kamchatka. I would need to make sure my medical supplies were topped off and that we would not have the benefit of the U.S. Coast Guard to come to our rescue in case of trouble as we would be well into Russian territory.

The *Northern Jaeger* was in Seattle undergoing some new modifications, so I'd be sailing with her from Seattle. This would allow me some time to get all my medical supplies inventoried and stowed before we started fishing operations.

The long voyage from Seattle to Dutch Harbor (seven days) was without incident. In Dutch, we took on the rest of the crew we'd need for our extended stay in Russia, and we quickly departed. We stayed within sight of the Aleutian chain of islands on our trip east.

The Aleutian Islands are a far-flung chain of more than three hundred small volcanic islands that sit on the edge of a subduction zone where two tectonic plates meet, similar to the Kamchatka Peninsula. At its deepest point, the trench is 25,200 feet deep or five miles. This region is ancient and has a wildness that will never accommodate subdivisions and strip malls. Viewed from the deck of a passing ship through the grey mist and fog, one feels as if they are looking upon a prehistoric landscape that has not changed or been altered in any way by humans since the dawn of time. This is the reason I chose to travel to the ends of the Earth, to see for myself these wonders. For me it is like a fresh breeze of cool mountain air coming into a room filled with smoke and confusion, overwhelming both with its purity and simplicity.

Coast of Kamchatka

For being so far away from civilization, these islands have a rich history both ancient and modern, from primitive peoples, European exploration by the likes of Bering, Cook, two World Wars, the Cold War and atom-bomb testing; yet their intense wildness shrugged all these off and remained defiant to human exploitation.

On the fourth day at sea, the coast of Russia came into view. The towering mountains of the Kamchatka Peninsula were like a massive fortress wall challenging anyone with thoughts of entering to think twice. I stepped out on the wing bridge to take some pictures and was instantly assaulted by the minus-thirty-degree temperature of the Russian winter. I never thought I'd be back there again. Remarkably to me, that coastline seemed even more wild and forlorn than the Aleutian chain had been.

Fishing operations soon began. Already I'd been at sea for almost three weeks. I was anxious to get the show on the road and fill our hold. It's funny how when you're back in the world after returning from a long voyage, the lure of the sea starts to tug at your sleeve and whisper in your ear. It can be confusing and a little tormenting at times because you remember how lonely, homesick, cold, and wet you were while you were out there and how all you wanted to do was go home. Yet the longing to return to the sea somehow manages to sneak its way into your thoughts no matter how miserable an experience you might have had. To this day, twenty years later, I've never been able to make sense of it.

There were half a dozen Polish crew members that were on board, friends of Henry's who had made their fateful leap to freedom years before with him. They were great to work with because they were incredibly hard workers that never complained. Like human machines, they were capable of enduring endless hours of excruciating work and pain that would have incapacitated lesser men. Since meeting Henry and observing these guys, I long ago had held them in high esteem.

So one night when I answered a knock at my cabin door and it was Dominick, one of the Polish crewmen on board, complaining of a terrible toothache, I knew immediately this could be serious. Of all the medical cases I could be faced with, I disliked dental emergencies the most. I had no dental training and no dental instruments on board. I'd take a heart attack any day before having to venture into someone's mouth.

He was in agony, near tears. I quickly led him to the cabin that was my makeshift hospital. There, before I did anything, I prepared an injection of pain medicine and injected it in various locations around the molar which I could see was infected and abscessed. I made Dominick comfortable in one of the bunks and explained that I'd be back shortly.

I ducked out of the infirmary and quickly made my way to the ship's office. From there I could contact Dr. Martin in Seattle for help on what to do next. There was always someone on radio standby in Seattle, so I was able to explain the situation. I was told to relax and wait for a reply that would be coming soon. A short time later, I was instructed to start an IV of amoxicillin (an antibiotic) and to draw a line around any redness or swelling taking place on Dominick's face. This would act like a baseline so I could keep track of any increase or diminishment of the swelling from thereon out.

I returned to the infirmary starting the IV drip of antibiotics and carefully outlining the little amount of swelling there was as instructed. At that point, there was little else I could do out there. It was a waiting game, hoping his symptoms wouldn't get any worse and stay manageable. I needed to let the captain know the situation in case it grew out of my control. After the antibiotic was administered, I turned in for the night.

When I awoke in the morning, I was anxious to see Dominick's condition. I dressed and peeked in on him as he slept. He was zonked out from the pain medication I had him on. When I took a look at him, I was shocked at his appearance.

Holy mother of God! The side of his face that the abscessed tooth was on had swollen to an unbelievable size. The entire side of his face from his forehead to his chin was bright red, well beyond the small baseline I had drawn the day before. I could not believe a living person's head could get so big. It was the size of a small basketball. Fortunately Dominick hadn't looked in a mirror yet. He was completely out of it.

I ran up to the ship's office and radioed Dr. Martin in Seattle. He was in this time. "Hey, how are you?" he cheerfully greeted me.

"Look, Doc, I'm fine, but I'm in a hell of fix here."

"OK, slow down and explain the best you can what's going on," he said.

Doing my best to sound professional and hide my panic, I explained the events as they had transpired. "This guy's head is the size of a watermelon, and we're out in the middle of nowhere."

I guessed he sensed my fear and very calmly instructed me to calm down, that everything was going to be fine, and I wasn't alone. "I want you to start orally giving him antibiotics, one every six hours for the next ten days. He should start to respond to the IV you gave him last night. It just takes a day or so for it to start attacking the bacteria, OK?" he asked.

"Yeah, sure, Doc. I can do that," I replied.

"Listen to me, we still have some time here before we have a real problem. You're just going to have to be patient and know you've done all you can for now, OK?"

Reassured, I let the waiting begin. In the meantime, I gave a full report to Tim, the captain. If Dominick's condition got worse, we'd have to stop our operations and speed toward American territorial waters to have the U.S. Coast Guard fly a helicopter out to us and pick him up. Every few hours now and then, I checked in on Dominick. When I saw him the next time only two hours later, his head looked like it was going to explode—it was so swollen. The only time I'd seen a human head this size was from a gunshot wound, and that person had died as a result.

It's unbelievable how much the body can expand and still remain intact. When someone swells that much they no longer look human but take on a monstrous appearance. Arms and legs can swell to incredible sizes. In the case of poisonous snakebites, the swelling can get so severe that incisions are made in the skin the length of the appendage to allow circulation to continue and save the limb.

Just when it looked like we would have to return to the United States later in the afternoon, I went to check on Dominick again, terrified at what I might see. When I took a look at him as he slept, I was surprised to see a noticeable reduction in the swelling and size of his head. I was amazed on how much the swelling and redness had dissipated. The antibiotics had finally kicked in, breaking down the bacteria's cell walls and sending the infection into submission. Man, was I relieved! I felt a huge weight lift from my shoulders, and I suddenly felt completely exhausted. Dominick still needed to see a dentist, but I had bought us several weeks or more of time, and maybe he'd make it the whole trip. Time would tell.

In the meantime, we sailed up and down the Kamchatka coast, setting our nets and hauling back nets containing fifty, seventy-five or sometimes close to one hundred tons of pollock. The finished products of surimi, fish meal, and fish oil were 25 percent of the gross weight brought in over the stern. So one hundred tons of whole pollock in the net equaled twenty-five tons of finished products; to me these numbers were staggering. We of course we not the only trawler out there fishing for pollock. In fact, there were eighteen others, all hauling in the same numbers.

I often wondered what it would look like if the Bering Sea were translucent and you could fly over it looking down. It seemed to me the sea would be packed with life of all kinds. I was told that schools of pollock can be ten miles wide and thirty miles long and thousands of feet thick and that hundreds of these schools roamed the Bering Sea. That doesn't include all the other species of fish such as the millions of salmon, cod, halibut, crab, and dozens of others all swimming just beneath waves. It was like comprehending the stars in the sky.

On one of my visits to the wheelhouse, I learned we were going to meet a Russian tanker to refuel, and at the same time meet a Japanese freighter to off-load what was in our freezer. We'd anchor in a cove along the coast, have one ship tie up on our starboard and the other on our port sides, and thus have fueling and off-load take place at the same time. We pulled up our net at set course for some distant spot on the map to meet the two vessels.

Kamchatka coastline, 1991

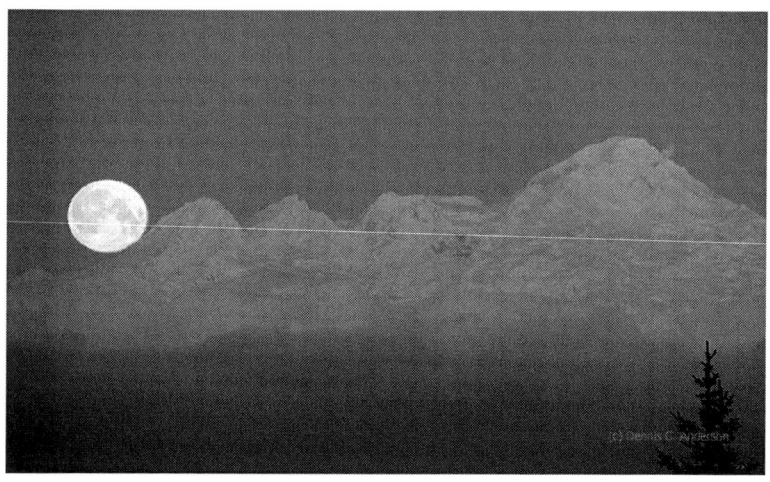

Moon over Kamchatka

During this time, we sailed very close to the shoreline. It was winter, with very short days consisting of many hours of twilight creating diffused and soft lighting. The massive volcanoes of the Kamchatka Peninsula were spellbinding in their beauty. Covered in a thick blanket of deep white snow etched against a crystal blue sky, many had active ash plumes rising in the frigid subarctic light. Later in the day, the sun would set behind this ancient landscape, creating a primal and surreal scene that could take your breath away.

Around four in the morning, we viewed a tanker at anchor ahead. There was a huge full moon floating over the mountains, illuminating the bay in silver moonlight. The captain skillfully brought the 337-foot ship gliding in alongside the tanker. Lines were thrown from our vessel, and we were tied up snugly alongside. The crew of the *Northern Jaeger* and the crew of the tanker lined the rails to peer at each other, our two decks separated by about twenty feet. Related by the sea yet vastly different, both groups stared at each other like people seeing a strange animal for the time.

Then the bartering and trading began, the spell of silence broken. In English and sign language resembling a game of charades, we began to trade. They were very interested in our jackets that were sold by the company that had our ship and company logo embroidered on the back; we in turn wanted fur hats.

Problem was, these guys were filthy. Life on a tanker was clearly a dirty job. Fuel oil coated everything, and everyone of them had their fur hats visibly stained with the foul liquid. Not to be denied, a few of their crew darted inside the ship and quickly returned with anything they thought might be a valuable souvenir. This included magazines, Russian money, jewelry, and flags.

The Soviet flag caught my eye as the Soviet Union no longer existed. I offered one of the crew holding up the red flag with the yellow sickle and hammer my *Northern Jaeger* jacket. He quickly made his way to the rail closest to me to make the exchange. This was done by having a large plastic garbage bag tied to a length of rope in which the articles to be traded were put into and then swung over to the other vessel. We made the exchange.

I had on my U.S. Air Force parka with a fur-lined hood, which all of them wanted to trade a fur hat for and which I wanted to do as well, except for the fact that all their hats were covered in fuel oil; and I wasn't going to trade my parka for one of those. Just about the time I was giving up on a fur hat, the captain of the tanker stepped out of the bridge onto the wing deck, wearing a beautiful blue fox fur hat in perfect condition.

When our crew saw this, the scene became like *The Price is Right*—everyone was shouting over to him, holding up jackets and hats, and waving money. Figuring I had just blown my opportunity for my Russian fur hat by just trading it for a flag, I was really disappointed. Then I noticed the Russian captain gesturing to one of us that he'd trade his fur hat. Everyone looked around to see who the lucky bastard was. After some confusion, it became clear that I was the lucky bastard; he wanted my parka. Damn, was I in luck. Without hesitation, even though it was ten degrees below zero, I quickly shed my coat and packed it into the plastic bag to be sent over to the tanker.

As soon as the Russians retrieved the parka, they put the coveted fur hat into the bag and flung it over to our deck. I couldn't have been happier. Immediately I was surrounded by our crew wanting to get a look at my treasure or trying to buy it off me with all kinds of monetary offers or trades for cameras or watches. I'd have none of it. I had made the best trade of the night and had no desire for anything other than my genuine Russian fur hat, much to the disappointment of my fellow crew members.

I stood my twelve-hour shift out on deck, inventorying pallets full of surimi as they swung over to the Japanese freighter that arrived shortly after our Siberian flea market had finished. I had to wear a company-issued freezer suit since I no longer had my parka, which I didn't mind at all because my beautiful Russian fox fur hat with the earflaps in the down position kept me quite warm in the subzero temperatures of the Siberian winter's day.

The Man Eater, Bering Sea, 1993

When the knock came on my door one night, I was in a deep sleep. I could hear the knocks as faint and faraway, drifting with beautiful white clouds in a crystal-blue sky. Then the knocks became louder and began to annoy me, distracting me from the wonderful scene unfolding before my eyes. Finally the knocks became very loud and fast, having a sense of urgency in them. I suddenly sat up in my bunk with a startled jerk, jumped out of my bed, and went to the door.

"What do you want?" I asked as if I really didn't know.

"You need to come to the factory. It's Tom. He's had his arm pulled into a Toyo machine. The engineers are taking it apart to try and get his arm out," a young, wide-eyed factory worker explained in a panicked voice.

"I'll be there in a minute. Let me get dressed," I answered.

Over the years, I'd come to expect anything out there, but as I quickly got dressed, I was having trouble trying to imagine the scene I'd find when I got there. I had to admit though that Tom would be at the top of the list for anyone who could pull something like this off.

Tom was not very educated, out of shape, overweight, unsightly with greasy hair, rotten yellow teeth; you get the picture. He was a hell of a worker and quite the character. Loud and boisterous, he was clumsy and accident-prone. I always have relied on my adrenaline to kick in at times like these, but for some reason as I made my way down to the factory, I was still struggling to pull out of the deep sleep I'd been in.

Still drowsy, I arrived at the scene of the accident. There was Tom standing next to the machine, his right arm completely pulled into it up to his shoulder.

A Toyo machine is an ingenious device invented by the Japanese that is full of spike wheels and spinning blades, conveyer belts, and gears that miraculously take in a whole fish in one end and spit out a headless, gutted open fillet out the other at a rate of hundreds a minute. The fish arrive at the opening of these machines in chutes and need someone to guide them in head first, where they're grabbed by a turning spike wheel with the sharpest points on the planet and sucked into the whirling machine.

Sometimes the fish become jammed at the entrance and need to be sorted out. A stick is used to flip the fish around into their proper positions. If the stick doesn't work, then the human hand is used (although it's against company policy). The writer of the policy, never having worked on a Toyo machine, didn't know it was impossible to keep a Toyo running at the speeds it ran at sea and not having to use your hand often to keep the whole factory moving smoothly.

The most common injury I treated on the vessel was from hands being sucked into Toyos, requiring anywhere from five to a dozen stitches on a person's finger or hand, determined by how far one's hand got into the machine before the quick action of the victim pulled it out of harm's way.

It seems that night slow and clumsy Tom managed to have his entire arm pulled into the machine, which I believe was and still is a first.

As I waited for the engineers to take apart the complicated machine, I was strangely detached from the bizarre scene before me. Tom was clearly in a lot of pain while two factory engineers frantically pulled piece by piece off the machine. Meanwhile the factory and all the people in it ground on with the never-ending work of producing surimi as if nothing out of the ordinary was going on.

When the outer cover was pulled off, you could make out Tom's arm through the maze of parts visible here and there, winding its way in seemingly impossible ways through the entire length of the strange contraption.

I started him on oxygen and cut away the sleeve of his free arm so I could get a set of vitals (heart rate, blood pressure) to establish a baseline. I also took the opportunity to start an IV using a large bore needle and line connected to a liter bag of saline solution in case he went into shock when his arm was extracted from the machine. I took a vial of the synthetic narcotic Stadol from my trauma bag and injected the required amount into the portal of the IV line to control his pain. This drug would not dilate Tom's blood vessels like morphine, reducing the potential for shock. The potential for serious, possibly life-threatening injuries existed as this machine had the capacity to seriously mangle his arm and sever major blood vessels.

As the time neared to extract his arm, my heart rate increased, and the adrenaline it was pumping began to kick in, lifting me out of my fog and into the reality of this situation. I readied several large trauma pads, gauze, and tape and had the stretcher brought down to the factory. I had Maria woken up and asked her to get the infirmary ready for pain control and stitching while I would treat Tom right at the scene for bleeding and shock.

Finally Tom was able to pull his arm out of the machine with help. All of us gathered held our breath for the ghastly sight we were about to see. Since he was wearing several layers of torn, shredded clothes and rain gear, at first it was difficult to see any injuries. Amazingly his arm was in anatomically correct position, which was a great initial sign. Everyone took a double look as it seemed impossible for his arm to emerge intact from such a twisted, powerful, and complicated machine.

I laid him down on the stretcher and immediately began to cut away the layers of clothes from his arm to get a look. As I did this, I could see his hand and fingers covered in blood, and several of his fingers looked mangled and clearly broken. As I exposed his arm, I could see black and blue bruising marks along the length of his forearm, from being pinched between the moving parts in the bowels of the machine.

I then came to a large gash on the top of his forearm, running lengthwise from just below his elbow down toward his wrist. Eight inches long, it gushed blood as it was freed from the constricting layers of clothing. I quickly laid a large thick trauma pad over the wound and wrapped it firmly with a roll of gauze then wrapped that with a roll of medical tape, making sure that it was applying pressure to the wound site.

Finishing that, I wrapped his hand the same way and treated him for shock by elevating his legs. Covering him in a warm blanket, I assigned some crewmen to take him up to the infirmary on the stretcher as I followed them up, mentally going over everything I was going to do next when we got there. Maria had everything prepared for us when we arrived.

Tom's vitals were stable, his bleeding under control, and pain managed. I unwrapped his hand to get a look at his fingers; three were in bad shape with multiple cuts and lacerations and were fractured in several places, causing them to bend at right angles in all the wrong places. His hand looked like ground hamburger in places, with flaps of skin and bloody tissue all mixed together.

After getting a good look at his injuries, I wrapped them again and explained to Tom that I was going to make a call to Seattle and speak with an orthopedic doctor to get advice on how I should best proceed and that I'd be back soon and to just relax. For him, his voyage was over.

Then I dashed up to the bridge and got on the satellite phone to Swedish Hospital in Seattle. With the help of Dr. Martin, I was able to speak with a specialist about Tom's hand. I described his injuries to the doctor, who listened carefully and asked me some follow-up questions. I took the time to explain to him that I had never treated an injury like this above the level I had already done.

He was calm and could sense my nervousness as he explained to me that Dr. Martin had spoken to him of my medical experience as an EMT III back in Seattle and how everything was going to be just fine. He understood me to be quite competent in my abilities and was confident I would successfully perform the necessary procedures.

He also told me how resilient human extremities were. He explained that I should set his fingers back into anatomical position to ensure circulation of blood to his fingers and then treat the lacerations, cuts, and flaps of skin. I needed to put everything back as closely to its original shape and position as possible using sutures, tape, and dressing to hold everything together. He said that I'd be surprised how well his hand would heal.

As I was working on Tom's hand, they'd be making arrangements for Tom to be airlifted off the ship by Coast Guard helicopter and flown to Seattle for ongoing treatment. Feeling a little more confident, I thanked him for all his advice and support and hung up. Then it was time to get back to the infirmary and earn my pay.

With Tom sedated and listening to music through earphones, I injected the numbing medication lidocaine into the nerve bundles located in the knuckles of his fingers above the lacerations, and I also straightened out his bent fingers. Then pulling the flaps of torn skin back into position over the bloody skin tissue with a few strategically placed sutures here and there, I was able to close the worst cuts and lacerations, bandage the rest then splint the fingers. The large deep cut on his forearm was cleaned.

All the while, Maria applied pressure to his brachial vein on the inside of his elbow to control the bleeding. Then I numbed the area, injecting lidocaine in and around the jagged wound and slowly began to close it using heavy gauge thread with a large fishhook needle to bring both sides of laceration together. When I was finished, his fingers, hand, and arm were a ghastly sight. Large, black and gnarly sutures stuck out all along the length of his swollen lower arm to his fingertips along with tape, splints, and gauze dressings. Tom was one lucky man.

I noticed huge nasty scars along his chest and stomach and asked him what had happened to him. He proceeded to tell me the story of how one summer's day in Seattle he had gone to a friend's house to get high. When he arrived, there was a man there he had never seen before, and they began to get drunk and smoke weed. Without any warning, the man got up and walked over to Tom and stabbed him in the abdomen with a large knife.

Shocked, dazed, and bleeding heavily, Tom staggered out to his car to drive himself to the hospital. On the way to the hospital, he decided to stop by his house which was on the way and get his pistol. He then returned to the scene of the stabbing, walked into the house, and shot the man who had stabbed him dead on the spot. Then returning to his car, he drove to the hospital where he collapsed in the ER.

He woke up three days later handcuffed to his bed. He recovered, was charged with manslaughter, and spent seven years in prison. As I finished treating him for his wounds, I thanked him for telling me his incredible story. He smiled, revealing his broken yellow teeth, "No problem, Doc. It's the least I can do for you taking care of me," he said.

With that he was helped to his room, his arm wrapped in a sling, to await his trip home. It had been two and a half hours since I was summoned to the factory. It was stressful, tedious work, requiring absolute concentration. As Tom was led out of the infirmary, I sat emotionally drained next to the bunk where I had treated him, my clothes splattered with blood. After a few minutes, I could feel the adrenaline wearing off, replaced with a growing feeling of how tired I was along with the realization of what a long, strange night this had been.

There is something about a voyage you are
barely aware of while you are making it.

—H. M. Tomlinson

Chapter 15

The Floating Town

In between the more serious cases I attended to at sea were the dozens of lesser medical problems I dealt with every day and night. The personnel dynamics working at sea on any fishing vessel are, number one, it's really hard work; and number two, there is a maritime law (the Jones Act) that states if you are injured at sea and must be returned to land, causing you to miss the rest of the voyage, you still will be paid for the full voyage even if you do not finish it.

This presents a set of circumstance in which some crafty individuals will try to fake illness or injury and be sent home early, only to get paid in full for the entire trip. Or at the very least, spend several days or more in their bunks unable to work as any time off is better than nothing. So the game begins, to try and filter out the persons who really are incapable of working or just faking it. This is not always as easy as you might think, and it's where medical experience can come in really handy.

Traditionally, before some fishing companies became more sophisticated and introduced EMTs on board, the captain was the medical officer. Most having limited medical training and having the huge responsibility of handling the ship and fishing operations, they found dealing with any medical problems a major pain in the ass. So unless you were on death's doorstep, no one dared approach a captain with any medical complaints or any complaints for that matter. A complainer was seen as weak and untrustworthy, thus scorned upon by fellow crewmembers. This resulted in abuses and lawsuits from those individuals who were indeed in need of medical care and were denied it. Also the treating of small medical problems before they became huge medical problems that ended up costing fishing companies large amounts of medical expenses unnecessarily.

Enter the state-certified EMT/crewman to the ranks of the few enlightened companies that fish the Bering Sea. Every day I had at least a dozen individuals come to me seeking a wide range of medical care, from headaches to heart attacks, from minor cuts to amputations, and everything in between. Then there was the mystery illness where the individual who was supposedly sick had no clue what his or her problem was, and neither did I. Every day, sometimes several times a day, these people would come to me complaining of pain and discomfort that seemed to migrate around the body, wreaking havoc on their bodies.

At first I went through the whole gambit of medical exams and treatments trying to pin down the mysterious disorder. Then one day, I had an idea in which to sort out the legitimate cases from the bogus ones; it turned out to be a stroke of pure genius. When one of these cases appeared, I would tell the unsuspecting person that I had some very special and powerful medication that I used very sparingly because it was expensive, and I only had a very limited amount. In their case, I was willing to use it reluctantly.

This special medicine was one of those large tablets, yellow or red in color (for effect), of nothing more than an antibiotic. For those of you who don't know, one antibiotic tablet is completely useless due to the way they work in the body. For antibiotics to work, the medication needs to be in one's system for at least several days to start working. The chemical molecules of the medicine attach themselves the bacteria's cell wall and begin to break them down. Once the protective cell wall is breached, the bacteria dies. As the number of bacteria cells die off, the infection slowly dissipates.

All this takes a few days and needs to continue until all the infectious bacteria are destroyed, or the infection will return. That's why when you get antibiotics from your doctor, they will tell you to take them every four to six hours for ten days even if you feel better before the ten days are up. So taking one antibiotic tablet does nothing for anyone, yet you would be astonished how many people I have cured with this wondrous drug.

The power of suggestion and the placebo effect we've all heard about is very real. I've seen it in action many times. The patient returns to me the next day feeling great and can't thank me enough for giving them my special medication. If on the other hand the patient continued to complain of symptoms, I would treat them to best of my ability usually convinced their complaints were real.

There was another trick I'd use, and I hate to call it a trick, but you have to remember, out there I could not afford to baby anyone. There simply was too much work to be done, and anyone not pulling their full weight put the burden on all the others who were doing their jobs. If the word got out that you could come to me complaining about anything and get a day off, the machine that was this vessel would break down very quickly. As a wise man once said, "If the machine breaks down, we all break down, and I can't allow that."

So the other method I used for complaints of pain was used in two different ways. First was the case of someone who had an illness or injury and had been off due to that injury and/or because of the strong pain meds they were on; they could not return to working around machinery while on the medication. This was a perfect situation to milk, using the "I'm in too much pain to work" angle for as long as possible.

So after a sufficient amount of time, I would think the patient's pain had subsided enough for them to return to work, but they would still insist that this was not the case. I'd switch from the usually narcotic medication to an ibuprofen without the patient knowing it then after sufficient time for the new medication to kick in, I'd ask the person how their pain level was. If they said the pain medication was keeping them pain free then I'd inform them they would be returning to work their next shift.

This would almost always be met with an angry response from the patient as they realized they had been tricked into revealing their deception. I'd then calmly explain that if the ibuprofen was sufficient to control their pain then they could to go back to work, sorry!

The other case was when someone insisted that they were in too much pain to work, that their pain was excruciating. As much as they'd like to work, they simply could not bear the agony then. Not knowing if this was truly the case or not and not wanting to put someone on a strong narcotic unless I really had to, I'd tell them that I was giving them something stronger than I really was, and I'd see what happened. More often than not the lesser pain med worked, and they would have to go back to work, pissed off that I had outsmarted them.

Because of my unique position as the ship's medic, I had access to the entire ship. Most of the factory workers were restricted from going to the bridge or engine room or the fish meal plant unless they had approval. Also there was a hierarchy on board most ships in which those lower on the chain did not mix with the higher on the chain. Because of my position, I mixed with the entire chain and knew everyone on board and mingled with everyone, from the lowliest factory worker from Vietnam to the chief engineer and the captain. I often found myself in the ghetto of the ship to the luxury condos.

As I stated earlier in the book, the *Northern Jaeger* was built originally to carry one hundred crewmembers. Due to the demands of surimi production, the actual number of crew needed was more like 180. This meant that spaces that were not originally intended to house people were changed to do so, spaces such as entertainment rooms that were designed for crewmembers to watch videos or read and socialize. These were stripped of everything: chairs, couches, shelves, and cabinets, everything except the sink; and mattresses would be placed right on the floor, and a dozen or more people would call it home.

Some cabins were constructed to fit six people, consisting of shelves with thin mattresses welded to the bulkheads. These were extremely cramped quarters and became very ripe for causing health problems as one could imagine as six people shared one hundred-square-foot room, all working various round-the-clock shifts seven days a week for months on end covered in fish slime all the while being tossed in every direction by an unsympathetic sea.

I'd be called here occasionally to take a look at someone ill or injured and was always a bit shocked at the conditions these guys lived in compared to mine. The *Northern Jaeger* was then a brand-new ship, so everything was clean and in good working order. The conditions I'm talking about were those created by a lot of men working long hours on different shifts in filthy factory conditions, all crammed into the same living quarters. Clothes and bodies can get ripe quickly. As everyone was always exhausted, washing clothes and taking showers usually were down the list of things to do.

Life on board most of the ships at sea except luxury liners and private yachts are a step down from the living conditions most of us have at home. That's a given unless you come from a third world country. Then on rare occasions life on an average ship can be a step up as was the case with our Russian observers on the *Royal Enterprise*.

On the other end of the spectrum was the officers' area. On the *Northern Jaeger*, this was located up on the superstructure of the ship. The captain, first mate, first engineer, VIPs, and I lived up there. In contrast to the middle-class two-man, four-man, and six-man rooms, and the ghetto below us, our rooms were huge. Mine was twelve by fifteen feet and had a bunk bed, a table with four chairs, closet, cabinet, shower, and toilet. The two-man, four-man, and six-man rooms had a door on either end of the shower/toilet room, so it accommodated two rooms of men. In the ghetto, there was no toilet in their room; so the guys there, as I witnessed on one of my visits, pissed in the sink and used one of the common toilets down the hall for their other business.

Those of us that could had a TV/VCR and/or stereo music player in our rooms as well. During our two months off, everyone recorded movies and favorite TV shows to watch while we were at sea; this was a godsend as it can get extremely boring at sea. This new technology made it bearable, and I often wondered how the people in past decades managed their boredom at sea. After one would watch all the movies they brought out with them then the trading began with other crewmembers. This almost always made it possible to watch a different movie every night after your shift was over, in the privacy of your own room.

For those crew members in rooms with a lot of people, they were left to having to watch whatever was on the TV in the galley. This usually was the same movie played over and over again for months on end yet somehow managed to entertain the masses of men from places other than the United States. As Americans, we were far too spoiled to watch the same movie over twenty times, so the galley was often full of the foreigners who always seemed quite content to be watching *Karate Kid III* for the third week straight.

Besides movies, food was the most popular entertainment and sought-after commodity on the ship. The *Northern Jaeger* had a huge state-of-the-art kitchen and always hired the best cooks available to run them. The food was always very good, and plenty of it was available. This made the long hours on shift and the endless days at sea tolerable, and as for me, after my experience on the *Royal Enterprise*, everything from thereon out for the rest of my life would be gravy.

Out of a crew of 180 or so, there would be on average five to ten women among them, again all from a variety of countries and states. It is an amazing thing how the presence of a woman in such dismal conditions can soften the roughest man's edges. I was always grateful to have at least one friend on board that was a woman and to be able to spend a little time during meals to talk to them. They brought a level of serenity into an otherwise noisy and mechanical world.

On a few occasions, there would be couples that managed to be hired and get a two-man room together. They were the envy of the rest of us for obvious reasons. For all sailors everywhere, the idea of having a girlfriend with you at sea was a universal dream that could never come true.

I had been called to the room of such a couple once during my years at sea. It seems they had a medical problem they were dealing with. For some time, they could not get a handle on solving it, so reluctantly I was asked to come see them in their room one afternoon.

The guy did most of the talking, explaining how he had developed a painful rash on his penis, which was by now very inflamed with open sores. I took his word for it as I wasn't anxious to see it for myself. He continued that he had passed the infection on to his girlfriend who was experiencing inflammation and pain and redness in her vaginal canal as well. Every time they made love, which they indicated was very frequent, the pain was almost intolerable. They desperately were looking for a remedy as they were suffering a lot of severe pain and discomfort.

I was amazed at the sacrifice they were willing to undergo for each other, and when I suggested the obvious, they were stunned at my recommendation: stop having sex until the rash was healed! I would give them an antibiotic skin cream for the rash and start them on a ten-day oral antibiotic schedule requiring them to take one antibiotic pill every six hours for ten days, and then I leveled the shocker: no sex until they were both completely healed.

Although they were willing to endure extreme pain making love to each other every chance they could, the idea of stopping to allow them the chance to heal was a real ordeal that took some convincing on my part. If not for me, then how about following my remedy for each other? When I put it to them like that, they slowly began to see the logic in my method and agreed to follow my advice. I left their room shaking my head, satisfied I'd solved another medical case, or had I?

As each day passed blurring into the other, the seemingly endless routine of work, sleep, work, and sleep became a real grind. One's world was reduced to a very tiny space consisting of a noisy, wet, miserable world of the factory deck, standing there for endless hours and performing repetitive movements surrounded by screaming machines and grey metal.

Then at the end of your shift, walking up a flight of stairs to a small stinky metal room stuffed with other crewmates getting ready for their shift and climbing into your bunk exhausted, only to get up in six hours and doing the whole mindless drill all over again and again and again.

This was how the days, weeks, and months passed at sea, often including periods of severe weather as the ship listed heavily from one side to the next, violently shifting position, lurching up, and plunging down the unseen waves, furthering one's exhaustion as you were forced to constantly brace yourself from being thrown from your station or pitched into the jaws of moving machinery.

Through all these, friendships were forged and enemies made. All the while the memories of home, family, friends, and loved ones never left your mind, producing a perpetual ache in your heart along with a steely determination not to fail them. Even now as you read this, they are out there somewhere producing the food the world needs, unappreciated and unknown.

How do you cure boredom? One word... adventure!

Chapter 16

Bombs Away

I was the first to see the plane. It was just a black speck against dark grey clouds, about ten degrees off our starboard bow. I was with Brooks, the *Northern Jaeger*'s first mate. He held a portable spotlight while both of us strained to spot the plane.

"There it is," I said as I pointed toward the speck on the horizon.

"Where? I don't see anything," Brooks responded.

"Just turn on the light and point in the direction I'm pointing. You'll see it soon enough," I shot back.

This episode started several days ago when the ship's purser, Mac, did not show up for his shift in the ship's office. Mac had become my best friend over the years of sailing on the *Jaeger*; he was mellow, down-to-earth, and soft-spoken. He lived in Mexico with his wife whom he had recently married. She was a Mexican national, and they had bought a house in a beautiful small town.

I worked with him when I needed to communicate to the mainland to send messages or speak to medical personnel in Seattle. I also went to him when I needed to order medical supplies. He was tall, thin, with curly black hair, a moustache, and goatee. He was educated and a semihippie, same as I was, and we soon found we had a lot in common. He was always on the six-to-six day shift, so when I made my daily visit to the office and someone else was sitting in for him, I knew something was wrong.

"Where's Mac?" was my predictable inquiry.

"He's sick in his bunk. He asked that you go and see him if you came in."

For Mac not to fill his shift, I knew this was serious. I immediately grabbed my medical bag and made my way to his room. I knocked twice and slowly opened the door to his cabin. It was dark and quiet. "Hey, Mac, are you in here?" I called out.

A soft, barely audible voice replied, "Yeah, I'm here. Come on in." I went over to his bunk finding him lying under his covers, just his head sticking out.

"What the hell is going on, Mac?" I asked.

"I'm sick as hell, my friend. I can't even get out of my bed."

"Why didn't you say anything to me?" I asked, irritated it had come to this without me knowing anything about it.

"Hey don't be mad. Look, you have your hands full already, and I felt I had a handle on whatever this is. I've been feeling lousy for several days. I thought it would pass, but I was wrong. This is kicking my ass," he explained.

"OK, let me check you out and see what I can figure out," I reassured him. With that I got down to a routine exam. I took his blood pressure and heart rate and asked him a series of questions, trying to get a lead on what this might be.

It wasn't until I was palpating his abdomen that I found my first strong indication of a possibility. As I pressed gently down on his abdomen over his liver, he let out a moan of pain. "For Christ's sake, man, take it easy on me."

"I'm finished. Let me do a little research on the information I have, and I'll get back to you soon. Just take it easy. I'll be back." With that I left immediately, going to my medical books I brought with me as a reference source. I had a gut feeling what it might be. I just needed to check out what the book had to say before I announced any diagnosis.

I found my medical encyclopedia and looked up hepatitis A; symptoms include weakness, nausea, lack of appetite, and pain in the abdomen due to inflammation of the liver. It was frequently found in third world countries due to the practice of using human fecal matter for fertilization and substandard sanitation infrastructure. Just what I thought. This did not prove he had hepatitis, but it backed up my suspicion enough to make up my mind this was indeed the case.

Mac would need to be sent to a hospital right away, so I went to the ship's office and called Dr. Martin at Swedish Hospital in Seattle to tell him of my findings and my conclusion. Once on the phone, Dr. Martin was skeptical of my diagnosis, doing his best to gently convince me it could be a host of other ailments and to relax and give it some time first. No matter how hard he tried to convince me otherwise, I stuck to my conclusion.

"Well, it's your decision, Erick, since you're there and I'm not. I'll respect any course of action you decide to take," he said.

"Thanks, Dr. Martin, I appreciate that. Since it has progressed to the point that he is bedridden, I'm going to make plans to get him to Seattle ASAP," I replied.

With that I headed up to the wheelhouse to speak with the captain. To get him off the boat, we would need to contact a vessel near us that was inbound to Dutch Harbor right away. Mac was severally dehydrated, and I would need to start him on an IV drip of saline solution in the meantime. On the way to the bridge, I checked my supply of IV bags. I only had one left—not enough.

I explained the situation to Captain Tim. He explained to me that if we were to do anything, it would have to be immediately as a severe storm was due within twelve hours; and once it arrived, it would prevent us from getting Mac off the ship until after the weather improved, which could be up to a week.

"Let's get started," I said. "I don't think Mac can wait another week to be treated." I remembered when I was on the *Northwind* twenty-five years ago. A crew member had come down with hepatitis, and several days after he was sent ashore, he had died. Any hesitation now could be fatal. Fortunately we found another trawler heading in to port near us, and arrangements were made to transfer Mac off the boat within hours.

I returned to inform Mac of the news. He was shocked to hear he might have a serious illness and of his sudden departure. As I hooked him up to a liter of saline IV, I assured him he'd be fine as soon as he got to the hospital. A few hours later, as the afternoon sky darkened with the approaching tempest, Mac was taken to an inbound trawler *Dynasty* in a Zodiac and was on his way home.

If I was wrong, it would be very embarrassing; yet I was comforted by the knowledge I had been trained with, that if I was to make an error in diagnosis, the error should be on the side of caution and not neglect. With that in my mind, I slept soundly that night knowing I had done the best I could for my friend and wished him well.

Several days passed, riding out another storm while deck operations continued around the clock. On one of my visits to the wheelhouse, Captain Tim handed me a memo received from Seattle a few hours ago. "You'll want to see this," he said, smiling and handing the paper.

It read that after several tests, it was determined that Mac did indeed have hepatitis A. He was immediately admitted to intensive care due to the advanced stage of the disease. He was in stable condition undergoing treatment. If he had not been hospitalized when he was, his long-term prognosis was grim, with death a real possibility. Also it had been determined to stop the possible spread of hepatitis on board the *Northern Jaeger*. Hepatitis A vaccines would be delivered to the vessel, and all crew members would be vaccinated as soon as possible.

I looked over to Tim when I finished reading the memo.

"Congratulations, Doc, looks like you might have saved Mac's life. How did you know he had hepatitis?"

"Truth is, Tim, I wasn't positive he did. Just an intuitive feeling I had based on the symptoms, that's all," I said.

"Well, there will be a plane coming out from Anchorage this afternoon. They're going to air-drop us 180 doses of vaccines and syringes. After we get them, you're going to have to vaccinate the entire crew, including yourself, OK?" he explained.

"Roger that, Captain. Let me know when the plane arrives, and I'll be ready."

Around four o'clock, word came that the plane carrying the vaccines was several miles out, requesting that we show a spotlight to ID us from the other trawlers in the area. Brooks and I headed for the bow. Brooks had the spotlight.

"There it is!" I shouted over the sound of the wind, pointing just off the starboard bow.

"Where? I don't see anything," responded Brooks.

"Just shine the light in the direction I'm pointing. You'll see it soon enough." Without another word, he switched on the powerful light and pointed in the direction I was pointing. The bow sliced into a wave, showering us with ocean spray. It was ice cold, and it caused us to crouch lower.

Soon Brooks shouted. "I see it! Good eye, Doc."

"They see us too. They're turning straight for us," I replied. Sure enough, the tiny plane dipped its right wing slightly, causing the plane's flight path to line up straight for us.

While this was happening, the ship's Zodiac was being lowered, with two deckhands to go out and retrieve the bundle of vital vaccines. It sped away from us a quarter-mile out and waited for the drop.

The speck got larger and larger until one could see it was a small twin-engine plane, the sound of its engines slowly becoming audible over the wind and waves. It made a low pass over us and gained a little altitude as it turned back around for its final pass. As it did so, it lowered its landing gear to slow its speed as much as possible before making its drop over the waiting Zodiac. Everyone stood silent, waiting for the moment the bundle would drop from the plane.

"Bombs away!" shouted Brooks as a tiny black speck appeared from under the belly of the plane. All eyes watched transfixed as the package fell from the sky.

With the precision of a bomber pilot, the package fell into the sea with a large splash only fifty feet from the Zodiac. The plane's engines surged with power as it struggled to gain power and speed, lifting its landing gear as it flew around one last time to confirm our pickup. The pilot flew one lower pass over us as the crew on the returning Zodiac and all of us on deck waved to signal success. The plane passed over tilting its wings up and down in the universal response and headed back to Dutch Harbor, slowly disappearing in the clouds.

Now it was time for me to go to work. I would vaccinate 180 people as each shift came off work. A long line formed outside my infirmary door. The processors worked six on and six off; the rest of the crew worked twelve-hour shifts. After twelve hours I finally finished. Rolling up my sleeve last after everyone had gone, I took a syringe full of vaccine with my right hand and injected my left shoulder with the serum. By now I had the touch, and it was painless; wish I could say the same for the first ten or so people in line who howled as I had injected them before I got it down. The serum was thick, and it needed to be injected slowly. Otherwise it created a strong, burning sensation which I learned about quickly.

As time went on, the rest of the crew relaxed as the sounds of pain subsided from the front of the line, and the word spread that it was painless. Exhausted, I had finished after working all night and previous day. Unfortunately it was now into my next twelve-hour shift, so it wouldn't be until six o'clock that night that I'd finally be able to sleep. Thirty-six-hour shifts were not uncommon, and after a strong cup of hot coffee, I was prepared for another day.

The Sea hates a coward
—Eugene O'Neill

Chapter 17

The Labyrinth Disease and the Heart

Sky over the Bering Sea

The years at sea passed with surprising speed. I was already an old salt by 1995. I had since moved to Alaska, and in the summer of 1995, I was married. Being away from my wife for months at a time made my time at sea much more difficult, and I knew deep in my heart, this lifestyle could not continue for much longer.

I had become a supervisor in the QC lab and had resisted all of the company's attempts to promote me even higher in the Quality Control ranks. I was a medic first; the world of a quality control technician on a trawler held no interest to me, much to the frustration of my QC supervisors. Emergency medicine was my first love and was why I returned again and again to the Bering Sea. I never knew what challenge the next voyage would bring, only that it would be something one could have never imagined.

This voyage would be no different. We were one hundred miles south southwest of the Pribilof Islands on routine trawling operations. I'd lost count of how many voyages I had made over the last five years. I was working in the lab located in the middle of the factory deck, surrounded by the noise and activity of a factory running at full capacity.

It was in the afternoon when the door of the lab swung open. The factory foreman, Lorie, stepped in with a look of cynicism on her face. Lorie was a tough woman, tomboyish as you might expect a woman to be, out there running a trawler factory. She didn't take crap from anyone and could stand her ground face-to-face with the toughest man.

"I've got one for you, Doc, out on conveyer number three, a real winner. Some guy complaining of dizziness and a headache. His name is Tony."

"Sounds normal to me," I replied. "Dizziness and a headache is how we all feel."

"Tell me about it, that's how I always feel," she answered.

"I'll check him out. What kind of worker is he otherwise?" I asked.

"He's usually no problem, does his work without any complaints. I think he's tired and wants some time off," she explained.

"Hey, how are you?" I said as I made my way up to him. He was soaked, standing in his rain gear next to a conveyer sorting out fish as they rolled by. He had a look of distress as he shook my hand.

"Hey, Doc, I'm not doing very well. I feel really strange."

Shouting out over the noise of the factory, I decided to have him come into the lab where I could conduct a proper exam on him. This was going to be tricky as I wasn't sure if he was faking or not. I needed a quiet place to speak with him as I wanted to be fair in my assessment as I could.

I noticed in the lab he was sweating heavily even though the temperature in the factory hovered around forty degrees. His eyes had a look of genuine confusion, concern, and stress. All these symptoms are hard to fake. "Try and give me something to work with," I asked. "You're giving me some pretty vague information, and I want to help you if I can," I explained.

"It's hard to explain, Doc. I can't put my finger on what's going on, only that something doesn't feel right. It's hard to stand, and I feel disoriented."

"From what you've been describing, you might be dehydrated. Come with me to the infirmary, and I'll get you started on a liter of saline solution IV." In the infirmary, I put a liter of fluid into him and gave him 500 mg of Ibuprofen and explained to him that he needed to drink plenty of fluids to stay hydrated and make sure he got as much sleep as possible. "That's all I can do for now, my friend. I hope this does the trick."

With that he was sent back to the line in the factory to finish his shift. I returned to finish my shift in the QC lab hoping I'd put an end to his problem. I was soon consumed with the responsibilities I had in the lab.

I'm on call 24/7, so I'm frequently woken up at all times of the night. By now, after many years on board, the foreman on duty knew not to wake me for every ache or pain reported. Those were endless and could wait until my next shift. At the same time, if they were presented with a situation they were unsure about, they should make any error on the side of caution as I was trained to do. It was always better to be safe than sorry.

At two in the morning came the knock on my cabin door. Light from the hallway streamed into my room as a head peeked around the door with the now well-known refrain, "Sorry to wake you, but you're needed in the factory."

Bag in hand, I made my way downstairs, my not-quite-awake senses assaulted by the suddenly overwhelming noise of the factory's never-ending grind of surimi production. Josh was waiting for me in the relative comfort of the QC lab. He was twenty-three years old from Portland, well built and in his prime.

"What seems to be the problem?" I asked.

"Well, Doc, I feel light-headed and nauseated, with some pressure in my chest." If Josh had been over fifty, I would have immediately focused in on his heart. Since he was a strapping young man in his early twenties, I figured maybe indigestion. Perhaps he'd need a spoonful of Pepto-Bismol. A little annoyed that I had been woken up for this, that's what I gave him along with some antacid tablets to chew on during his shift.

He went back to the line, and I made my way up the bridge to check in with Brooks who was on the night shift in the wheelhouse. I told him of the two guys I'd seen. His typical response was that they were faking it and I'd done a good job putting them back to work. I nodded in agreement, but as an experienced EMT, I knew in the back of my mind that things weren't always what they appeared to be at first glance. I wasn't convinced these two guys were the type to fake an illness to get out of work. After some small talk, I returned to my room and fell asleep.

In the lab, the next day at noon, Lorie came into the lab informing me that Tony had not made it to his shift and was up in his bunk claiming he was unable to get out of bed. Damn, if this isn't what I hated to hear. What have I got on my hands? With a sense of urgency, I quickly made my way to Tony's room. There I found him curled up in his sheets moaning in misery.

"What the hell's going on, Tony? Talk to me." Through the moans and tossing and turning, he told his story of waking up and feeling like he was falling out of his top bunk with the room spinning and a growing sense of nausea. He continued to explain that every time he opened his eyes the room would start spinning and he'd start to throw up.

OK, I had to think hard what could this be. During the night, the seas had risen, and we were rolling and listing pretty good. *Could he be seasick? What else could it be? Come on, think.* My brain was racing, going over all the medical training I'd had over the last seven years, trying to match these symptoms to a possible illness. Maybe a stroke, but that was highly unlikely for someone in their thirties. I was drawing a blank.

"Can you stand up for a moment so I can try and get more information from you?" I asked. "Come on, I'll help you," I encouraged him. I reached up, put my arms around him, and lifted and pulled at the same time, dragging him out of the top bunk.

As soon as his legs touched the floor, he collapsed in a heap and vomited. Tony was a pitiful sight slumped on the deck like a pile of dirty sheets, surrounded by his vomit that sloshed back and forth across the floor with the motion of an agitated sea outside.

OK, I guessed he was not faking this. He lay there moaning, completely limp. Doing my best to help him reclaim some of his dignity, I reached down under his shoulders and in one mighty lift, I half lifted, half flung him onto the bottom bunk that was empty. The person who slept there was on shift in the factory. I lifted his dangling legs up onto the bunk and grabbed a towel hanging on the back of the door and started wiping up the vomit from around his mouth and side of his head all the while holding back my own body's desire to vomit from the stench.

All right, it was pretty clear we had a problem. If he was seasick, it was the worst case I'd ever seen, and in my gut I didn't believe it was going to be that simple. I made him as comfortable as possible and made my way to my medical library I had created over the past several years in the infirmary. There I had collected a dozen medical reference books along with my books on treating trauma and heart attacks.

One in particular had become a favorite over the years, helping to correctly diagnose a variety of cases I would have otherwise not been able to treat without the invaluable information I was able to get from its pages—the American Medical Association's *Encyclopedia of Medical Symptoms and Treatment.* What I had learned years ago was that if you didn't know something off the top of your head then you needed to know where to find the information quickly.

Let's see. Disorientation, nausea, room spinning, unable to keep one's balance—flipping through the pages of the thick, heavy book, I slowly I caught two words that sparked my interest. At the top of a page in bold letters was "labyrinth disease." It was a viral infection of the inner ear that affected the semicircular canals, three loops of fluid-filled tubes attached to the cochlea in the middle ear that help maintain the sense of balance; symptoms include loss of balance, intense vertigo, sensation of uncontrolled spinning, nausea, headache, diaphoresis (sweating), and a sense of general unease.

The instant I read this definition, I knew I'd found the problem. What a stroke of good fortune. I was elated and immediately made my way to the ship's office to get off a report to Dr. Martin in Seattle. After I did that, I made my way to the wheelhouse to inform the captain of the events that had been transpiring over the last twenty-four hours. I realized that I could not treat this out there, and Tony would have to get back to Anchorage as soon as possible. Explaining all this to the captain, it was clear we would need to find a vessel heading back to Dutch and transfer Tony to it to get him back for treatment.

The captain, not completely convinced he was not faking it or thought he just had a case of seasickness, had over the years come to trust my judgment largely because I had never been wrong, yet! I had my fingers crossed that my record would not change with this exotic diagnosis.

Until we could get Tony safely aboard an ingoing ship, he was my patient, and it was my responsibility to see to his needs; so I returned to his room and finished cleaning up the mess made earlier then made arrangements for the person that was sleeping in the bottom bunk to move to the top bunk. Then I went back to the office to see if I had a reply from Seattle; to my relief, I did.

Dr. Martin in classic doctor form doubted my diagnosis and for the life of him could not figure out how I could have come up with such a rare and obscure one at that. Yet at the same time, he also had come to value my gut feelings and had long ago deferred to my judgment at sea and did so again this time as well. He would make arrangements for Tony's arrival in Anchorage. In the meantime, since Tony hadn't eaten in the past day and had been vomiting, Dr. Martin suggested I give him a liter of fluid IV to replenish his fluid needs and ward off dehydration. I agreed and set off to do that.

I was informed that it would be another day before we would meet up with another trawler heading in to Dutch Harbor, so I began my round-the-clock vigil on Tony. I had to try and get some food into Tony to keep up his strength, so I had to spoon-feed him soup. Also he could not stand on his own let alone walk and since he lived in a room where the toilet was down the hall, I had to assist/carry him to the bathroom whenever he needed to go. This was a daunting task as the seas were rising in intensity, making it difficult for a normal person to walk.

Tony was in a terrible state, and I really felt for him. Anyone who has spent a day at sea knows that it is not the place to be if you were suffering from disorientation, dizziness, and nausea as being at sea is synonymous with these feelings for the healthiest of people. Every time he had to go to the head (the name for toilet on a ship), his misery factor would go through the roof, moaning and crying and slumping to the floor; all the while I tried to hold him up while both of us were tossed from one bulkhead to the other by the heavy seas in the narrow hallway.

Several times in our thirty-foot journey, I had to reach under his arms and lift him off the floor, throwing one of his arms over my shoulder and carrying him a few more steps until he could stand no more of the conflicting motions; and he'd collapse in my arms, ending up in a heap on the hallway floor, making sounds like a dying animal. Reaching down again, we'd repeat this process all the way to the head and back to his bunk, several times a day and night. As you might have sensed here, the life of an EMT is not all glamour and glory. There's a lot of dirty work and body fluids that can cause you to question at times if you'd made the right career choice.

As I lay fast asleep in the bunk above Tony, that knock at the door came again. I had had only an hour here and there of sleep over the past thirty hours and was completely exhausted both physically and mentally.

"Hey, Doc, wake up! Hey, Doc, *wake up*!" came the distant voice as I emerged from my deep sleep. "Josh has passed out in the factory. Come quick!"

Staggering down the hallway, I struggled to get my brain engaged for the next drama that was quickly unfolding. I had completely forgotten about Josh and having not heard anything more from him, had put him out of my mind. As I raced down hallways and downstairs, I had no idea what to expect next.

By the time I reached the factory where Josh worked, he was conscious and still, lying on the factory floor surrounded by several crewmembers. I quickly checked to see if he was breathing OK and if he had any bleeding. I then instructed one of the guys standing nearby to get our stretcher from the infirmary and bring it there. While he went to do that, I used the time I had to get the blood pressure and heart rate and to question Josh on what was happening with him.

He was covered in sweat and pale as a ghost. His blood pressure was normal, but when I felt for his pulse, I detected an irregularity in the beat of his heart. He explained that he had had dizzy spells and moments of light-headedness over the few days and had experienced a spell when he blacked out. All these symptoms were known to me and were the classic symptoms of a heart problem. I was confused though because these were symptoms of someone usually thirty years older than Josh.

I had no choice but to ask the obvious question. "Do you have a history of heart problems?"

I was taken aback when he calmly answered yes.

"You have a history of heart problems?" I asked again.

"Yes, I have had problems in the past similar to this. I was hospitalized for it two years ago," he replied.

"Why didn't you tell me this sooner? Josh, for Christ's sake, do you have a death wish?" I said. I was incredulous at him leaving out this critical information. His response was that he didn't want to lose his job and hoped it would pass without becoming a problem.

By then the stretcher had arrived. He was gently placed on it, and I had him carried up to the infirmary where I placed him on oxygen and stripped him of his rain gear and wet clothes and made him comfortable in a bunk.

"OK, Josh, just relax, and take it easy. All your vital signs are stable, and I'm going to make sure you're taken care of. I'll be back soon with more information. Just sit tight."

I went immediately to the wheelhouse. I needed to place a call to Seattle as I couldn't wait for a fax. I explained the situation to the captain. As I waited for the call to go through, Dr. Martin patched me through to a heart specialist at Swedish Hospital in Seattle. I explained to him that I believed the arrhythmia (irregular heartbeat) in Josh's heart was preventing his heart from contracting strongly enough to pump oxygenated blood throughout his body, causing him to black out.

The doctor quickly agreed, and we both acknowledged the urgent need to get Josh to a hospital ASAP. A transfer to another ship was going to be to slow; what we needed was a helicopter pickup. Captain Tim was a bit shocked by the rapid development of events and was a bit in denial at the seriousness of the situation.

"He's had too much coffee, that's all his problem is. Doc, you really think he needs a goddamn helicopter?"

"Yeah, I don't *think* he needs a helicopter. I *know* he needs a helicopter, and so does the heart specialist in Seattle. Sorry."

"What the hell? I already have another trawler transferring Tony, now I need a helicopter too?" He continued to rant as he picked up the radio microphone to call the Coast Guard base on Kodiak Island.

"You'd better be right about this, Doc, or you're going to be in a world of shit with the company, you understand?"

A moment of doubt ensued. Hearing those words, I froze in my tracks contemplating my decision. Then in an instant, the doubt passed. I was positive in my decision. If I was to make a mistake, it had to be on the side of caution for Josh and his well-being, not mine. I'd take what consequences may come my way if I was wrong.

Just then the ship's phone rang. Captain Tim answered. "It's for you, Doc. Tony fell out of his bunk and is moaning on the floor."

I grabbed the phone. "Will you please get him back into his bunk? I'll be down there as soon as I can, for Christ's sake!"

I slammed down the phone and looked over at Tim. He burst out laughing. "You've got your hands full now, Doc. Calm down, everything's going to work out fine. I've got your ship and your helicopter on the way. Need anything else? Maybe a submarine?"

"Very funny. No, I don't think I need a sub, at least not right now. Thanks, Tim," I answered. I turned and left the bridge, heading back down to check on Tony and then get back to Josh.

When I arrived at Tony's side, he was back in his bunk. He had been trying to get himself to the head when he fell. So I helped Tony to the head and back to his bed; exhausted from that, I made my way to the infirmary to check on Josh.

His color had returned due to the oxygen. He was still short of breath, so I arranged his pillows so he could lay in his bed in more of a sitting-up position. With his heart not contracting as strongly as it should, it could cause blood to back up into the lungs, making it difficult to breathe.

Josh would be the first to go. The deck crew was alerted to the pickup, and when the time came, Josh was dressed and fitted into a Mustang Survival Suit for the lift. Having regained his strength, he was able to walk aided by me up to the bow. The noise and wind from the hovering helicopter was almost overpowering, along with the ship slicing through the waves, sending freezing spray over the bow. It was downright miserable.

The crew of the helicopter tossed out a line attached to the basket, establishing a ground between them and the ship. A tremendous amount of static electricity is produced by the hovering helicopter, and without a constant ground, anyone touching the recue basket could be electrocuted. It was pretty exciting having a large helicopter hovering forty feet above you with its rotor wash blowing you almost off your feet while you're trying to get someone into a tiny swaying basket as the deck of the ship lifts up and then plunges down the side of waves and freezing salt spray soaks you with ice-cold water all the while doing your best not to be electrocuted. Slowly Josh was lifted up into the helicopter, and it soon disappeared in the distance.

Soon after, word came that the trawler *Triumph* would be meeting us. Tony was next. It was decided that I'd go over on the Zodiac with Tony to fully explain to the crew of the *Triumph* of Toni's strange condition and all that was needed to care for him while en route to Dutch. I hadn't slept in over twenty-four hours and was anxious to get Tony off our ship and on his way.

Time came to load up Tony, and the same drill with Josh was done to prepare Tony for his boat ride. I cannot tell you how sorry I felt for Tony; any motion caused him tremendous amount of misery. The infection of his middle ear affected the part of the ear responsible for balance and our feeling of orientation on this planet. With that out of whack, vertigo sets in, causing major disorientation. The worst place on Earth he could be right at that moment was on a ship on the Bering Sea and then taking a trip on a small rubber Zodiac raft over to another ship.

The sounds he made were not human and often sounded like a gut-shot cougar. He had to keep his eyes closed to keep from going insane with motion sickness, and it was heartwrenching to watch a man suffer so much.

He was lifted into the dangling Zodiac, and I jumped in and took my place as we were slowly lowered in the waiting sea. The *Triumph* was positioned about three quarters of a mile off our bow. The sea conditions that day consisted of large, very large rolling waves. These did not break but were wide and high and rolling waves.

The Zodiac' was timed to be released as the peak of one of these twelve-foot rollers rose up to just beneath the hull of the tiny Zodiac. The timing was perfect; and as we touched down on the water, we immediately slid off the side of the wave into the trough below, kicked in the small but powerful outboard motor, and were on our way over to the waiting trawler.

If one felt small on a three-hundred-foot ship in the middle of the Bering Sea, there are few more humbling experiences as being in the middle of the Bering Sea in a fifteen-foot rubber boat. We rode up one side of the massive rollers like making the summit of a small mountain then slid off the side down into the valley between, the sensations being exactly like on a roller coaster when you were a kid. The awareness of your tininess in this universe and the immensity of the raw nature that surrounded you was inescapable and profound, one that I'd never forget.

The entire trip over, Tony was curled up in the fetal position on the deck of the Zodiac moaning out strange and eerie sounds, unnerving myself and the crewman steering the Zodiac. We were soon lifted up the side of the *Triumph*, and we lifted Tony from the small boat. We were directed to his room where he was undressed and put to bed. He thanked me for all I'd done for him, and I wished the best. I then made my report to the captain and made my way back the Zodiac. We were lowered and made our way back the *Jaeger*. I then made my way up to our wheelhouse and made my report to Tim.

"Nice work, Doc. I'm sure glad you're here, and I didn't have to deal with that circus. Is that it for now?" he asked.

"Goddamnit, I sure hope so," I replied, exasperated.

He laughed. "Go get some sleep. I'll let the QC lab know you'll be there for your next shift. Until then, relax and again, good work."

The pessimist complains about the wind;
the optimist hopes it will change; the realist
adjusts the sails.

—William A. Ward

Chapter 18

An Arm and a Leg

Aleutian Islands

On this voyage in the summer of 1995, we were operating along the western Aleutian Islands within sight most days of Attu or Kiska Islands. These outcast specks of land had been the site of the only land battles fought on American soil during World War II. No matter how remote or barren these islands were, they were American soil. No matter that their occupation had little military or strategic value for the Japanese, Americans were not going to let their invasion of these islands stand.

On May 11, 1943, eleven thousand U.S. troops landed on Attu. Bitter fighting through May and a Japanese banzai charge on May 30 left one thousand Americans and two thousand Japanese dead at the end of the battle two days later. Thirty-five thousand U.S. troops landed on Kiska on August 15, 1943, only to discover that the Japanese had evacuated under the cover of dense fog. That ended the only occupation of foreign troops on American soil since 1812. Staring out from the warmth of the *Northern Jaeger*'s wheelhouse, it was hard to imagine anyone fighting a war way the hell out there in the godforsaken middle of nowhere

We had been at sea on this contract for thirty-five days and had off-loaded in Dutch once our freezer hold was already half full again. I had just received a fax from Seattle with an update on Josh's condition. Captain Tim handed it to me with a big smile, so I figured the news was good.

He had reached the hospital in Anchorage only six hours after he was picked up by helicopter. When he arrived, they found his heart was twice its normal size, swollen from the backup of blood and pressure from its inability to pump because of the irregular beats. The letter said that if Josh had not reached the hospital when he did he would have most likely died within twenty-four hours.

When I finished reading the note, I looked up at Tim. He was beaming. "Nice work, Doc, looks like you did it again."

We weren't on any record-breaking pace by any means, but we were doing OK. Tim, our captain, had long ago established the reputation of being able to find the fish and fill a freezer with uncanny consistency. We had always outperformed the other boats, the *Northern Hawk* and the *Northern Eagle* as well as most of the other eighteen or so trawlers in the surimi fleet at that time. That translated into earning more money over a year's period, making the *Northern Jaeger* the ship to be on.

We had a tight crew with most of the same people coming back over and over again. After several years, we'd become a team and developed into a highly efficient crew. The trawlers that struggled to fill their freezers had a high turnover rate and were always in the process of training a green crew and weeding out slackers, constantly hampered with inexperience and poor performance. Their bottom line suffered.

As I've mentioned before, we had a half dozen or so Polish crewmen on board. You've met several of them earlier in the book. They were a big reason our crew was so good. Peter was one of the Polish crewmen. He worked in the freezer hold. This in itself speaks volumes to his strength and character. He was a big man, not fat in any way, just built large. Around six foot and weighing in at 250 or so, he had a beard which was always frosted over with ice from spending endless hours working at thirty degrees below zero.

The *Northern Jaeger*'s freezer hold was enormous, built to hold sixty-five to seventy thousand cases of surimi. It was the freezer hold crew's job to stack and fit each case precisely not only so that we could fit that many cases in the space allotted but also in a way that did not risk the safety of the men working down in the freezer.

Remember this freezer rocked and listed with the unpredictable moods of the Bering Sea. Each case was shaped like a domino, maybe eight inches thick and three feet long, eighteen inches wide and weighing forty-five pounds each. They were capable of being stacked forty feet high and when frozen solid had the consistency of a concrete block.

As they reached the end of the processing stage in the factory, they were stacked onto one of two large freight elevators and sent down to the freezer one hundred at a time. There they were placed on movable conveyer belts that took them to whatever section of the freezer hold was being filled at the time.

This was a science and had to be done with absolute precision. Several men waited at the end of the belts, and when a case reached the end, it was lifted and fit into place like a brick being placed into a wall. The cases came in a steady pace hour after hour. The work building the stack was backbreaking and relentless. Wearing thick overall freezer suits, the men endured the severe, numbing, frostbite-producing cold while lifting thousands of pounds of surimi per shift in a constantly moving environment day after day, week after week, month after month.

The Arm

This was where Peter worked ever since I could remember. For this feat, I had tremendous respect for the man. He was a gentle giant, always happy, quiet natured and respectful; so when a crewman burst into the lab wild-eyed and frantic, blurting out that Peter had been crushed by a stack of surimi in the freezer hold, I was momentarily stunned. Then a surge of adrenaline flushed into my veins, and I grabbed my trauma bag and raced for the freezer stumbling the entire way, trying to get on a freezer suit I was handed while half walking, half running to the hatch that led down to the freezer hold.

I knew this was going to be bad as I slipped into the manhole hatch and began climbing down the forty-foot ladder. Shocked at the intense change in temperature as I descended, I struggled to get my mind focused on what I was going to see when I reached Peter. What's happening in your mind at moments like these is kind of a controlled panic as a flood of emotions and thoughts swamps the brain in the few moments you have before reaching the scene. You're in a mad scramble to sort your mind out and get all your thoughts prioritized so you can function when you arrive. Also you're scared to death and are fighting to get your fear under control, knowing all eyes are going to be on you expecting you to take control of the situation.

I reached the bottom of the cavernous hold and was directed to a section of the freezer that had a noticeably different appearance than the rest of the neatly stacked, right-angled world of a freezer hold. I could see a jumbled mountain of surimi cases ten feet high that was clearly out of place and instinctively made my way over to it. A small group of blue freezer-overall-clad men gathered around Peter sitting slumped over next to the pile. He was conscious, which was a great sign as he easily could have been dead. He was holding his right arm guarded with his left arm across his chest, slumped over, moaning and slightly swaying back and forth.

I knelt down next to him, bringing my face close to his to speak to him. When he looked at me, he was white as a ghost. "How bad are you hurt, Peter?" I asked, looking him straight in the eyes.

"I think I broke my arm," he replied, grimacing with pain as he spoke.

I looked up at the men gathered round. "Did he lose consciousness at any time?" I asked.

"No," they responded. That was excellent news.

OK, first things first. I quickly checked for major bleeding, difficulty breathing, and his level of consciousness. All good. Next I needed to get him out of the freezer right away and treat him for shock, so I needed to get him someplace warm immediately. I sent a runner to get a stretcher while I laid Peter down on a flat stack of surimi cases. I stacked a few cases at his feet and lifted his legs up onto them, elevating his legs to help keep his blood at his body core in an effort to keep his blood pressure up. I quickly performed an examination of his body the best I could, through his thick layer of clothing, to assess any other injuries he might have.

I placed both hands around first one leg then the other and ran them up pressing along their length for any signs of deformities or reaction of pain from Peter. Then I palpated his abdomen and chest, then arms, and finally his head. Other than his right arm, he appeared not to be seriously injured. Outwardly I could not be sure of any internal damage he might have until I got a closer look at him topside.

The stretcher arrived. He was placed on it, and we carefully made our way over to the elevator. We were raised to the factory level and carried Peter up the stairs to the infirmary. From there he was placed on a bed. I thanked everyone who had help get him there and dismissed them and got to work getting Peter out of the many layers of clothes he had on.

As soon as I finally got his freezer suit and gloves off, I could begin to see the extent of injuries to his arm; they were severe. I cut off his long underwear top and shirts, seeing then his forearm was deformed and clearly broken in more than one place. There was a laceration midforearm where his arm took on an unnatural angle. It was two inches long and was bleeding steadily. When I looked closer, I could see the jagged white end of his radial arm bone just below the skin. This is what is called an open fracture, caused when a bone is broken and then punctures the skin, exposing the bone.

His right hand was swollen, and four of his fingers were severely broken with each one having several unnatural angles. Also there were several jagged cuts on his hand and lower arm caused by a crushing force. They oozed blood and were several inches long. There was a lot of bruising and redness to the surrounding skin and tissue. All in all, his right arm and hand were severely injured by hundreds of pounds of surimi cases falling on them.

All this time, Peter had remained quiet other than an occasional moan. I reassured him he was going to be fine and was relatively lucky to have come out of this accident with only the injuries he had. He reassured me that he knew I'd take good care of him as his friends Henry and Dominick had spoken highly of my care of them in the past.

I then had a lot to attend to. First was getting the bleeding under control, which I did by wrapping each cut with gauze. Then pain control; first I got his vital signs such as heart rate, breathing, and blood pressure. With a strong blood pressure reading, I could start him on an IV morphine drip, which I set up. He needed a good, strong blood pressure to start him on morphine as morphine causes the veins and arteries to dilate, which can cause a drop in BP. Shock also causes the veins to dilate as well, further lowering blood pressure. A low BP is not good.

So far I had everything under control. Peter was stabilized and resting comfortably. Then I needed to report to the captain and to Dr. Martin in Seattle to come up with a plan of action.

Tim had already been notified of the accident when I arrived in the wheelhouse. He asked me what the damage to Peter was.

"He's extremely lucky. He has an open fracture to his right arm, a crushed hand, and four broken fingers, with several large cuts on the hand and arm as well. Other than that, he is fine."

"That's lucky?" Tim replied.

"It is if you saw the twenty-foot mountain of surimi cases that fell on him. It's damn lucky!" I replied. "Now we just need to figure out what to do with him," I continued.

"Well, there isn't any way we can transfer him to another boat, if that's what you're thinking, Doc. We're all alone out here in this part of the woods," Tim explained.

We were four miles off the coast of Attu Island in the western Bering Sea. The rest of the fleet was hundreds of miles further east. Tim had decided to follow the beat of a different drummer this trip and fish the species of pollock that inhabited this remote part of the Bering Sea.

"Can you get me Seattle on the satellite phone, Tim? I need to speak with Dr. Martin right now on what to do with Peter's open fracture."

A few minutes later, I was on the phone with Dr. Martin and explained the entire situation to him. "You need to get him to a hospital in Anchorage as soon as you can," he explained.

"Roger that," I replied, "But how? We are way the hell out in the middle of nowhere."

"There's a naval base on Adak Island relatively close to where you are," he said. "I'll call you back as soon as I get a number, so you can reach the base," and he hung up.

"Adak—how far are we from there, Tim?"

"Adak? That's around five hundred miles from us," he replied. "Do we have to go to Adak?" he continued.

"Possibly. That's the best we can do. It's not that bad, Tim. That's only a forty-eight-hour run, and we can start fishing off Adak after we drop him off, can't we?"

"Well, yeah, I guess we can. I'll call you up when I hear from Seattle. You'd better check on Peter," he replied.

I returned to the infirmary and reexamined Peter's arm. The lacerations on his hand and arm were still bleeding and had soaked through the dressings I had on. The color of the blood was dark red, and it oozed out in a slow but continuous flow, indicating to me damage to veins. I also noticed his arm and hand swelling, doubling in size.

I was instructed to set his broken fingers by Dr. Martin, so I gathered the necessary equipment and supplies. To numb his fingers, I used injections of lidocaine in what's known as a digital block. By injecting the analgesic lidocaine into a knuckle above the area to be worked on, all the area below the injection site will become numb. I made the necessary injections and proceeded to straighten out his bent fingers. Grabbing on the end of one of the fractured fingers, I pulled hard, straightening them out one at a time then splinting them together for mutual support.

I checked to see if he had a pulse in his wrist, making sure the fractured arm that was bent had not pinched off the flow of blood to his hands and fingers. I also performed capillary refill on his fingernails to show me blood was reaching his fingers. This is done by squeezing down on his fingernails and then releasing the pressure and observing how long it takes for the nails to turn from white to pink. It should take no longer than two seconds. His blood flow was good.

The swelling of Peter's arm was beginning to alarm me, so I decided to ice his forearm and hand using damp towels filled with ice. I sat and made small talk with Peter, removing the ice packs every five minutes or so for the same amount of time then repeating the process. I was used to spending maybe thirty minutes with patients back home, working 911 calls. After that they'd be in the care of an ER staff.

I hadn't experienced the amount of swelling a crushing injury can produce. Quarter-size blisters were appearing on the skin which was bright red and purple by now. As the swelling increased, it opened up the cuts on his arm and hand and increased the internal pressure, making it impossible to stop the bleeding. Every half hour, I needed to change the blood-soaked dressings.

While I was growing more and more concerned about the changing shape of Peter's arm, he remained calm and reassured me he'd be fine. I was afraid that at some point the swelling would become so great that it would cut of the flow of blood to the damaged area. If that accorded out here, he could lose his arm. At a hospital, they could perform a procedure where incisions are made lengthwise in the skin with a scalpel, laying open the skin and reducing the pressure on the blood vessels. I did not want to have to do that out there in these conditions by myself, yet I knew we were in a race against time.

Finally the phone rang. It was Tim letting me know he had the radio frequency to Adak's commanding officer and for me to get topside right away. I wasted no time and was in the wheelhouse in moments. First I called Dr. Martin in Seattle using the satellite phone. Then I had Tim use the ship's radio to make contact with the naval base; and after a few minutes, I had the commanding officer on the radio, and our teleconference began.

I quickly explained our situation to the CO at Adak. He didn't waste any time explaining that Adak Naval Station was a restricted area even to other military personnel and that he could be of no help to us. I repeated the CO's words into the satellite phone to Dr. Martin, holding the phone to my ear with my right hand while I spoke to Adak with the radio I held in my left hand.

Dr. Martin quickly told me to ask Adak if there were any conditions at all they would allow Peter to come ashore, which I did. The CO's next question was, was Peter an American citizen? I already knew he was not; he was a Polish national. My heart sank.

There was a pause at the other end of the radio then came the static reply, "This is a highly restricted frontline military installation. No one is allowed to enter except for the possibility of the loss of life or limb and then only, I repeat, only if they are an American citizen. Do you copy, *Northern Jaeger*, over?"

"I copy that, Adak. All we are asking for is a flight to Anchorage to save a man's arm. I can assure you this man is not a spy or a security risk of any kind. I've known him for many years. Please reconsider your last transmission, over."

"Stand by, *Northern Jaeger*, over."

"Roger that, Adak, standing by."

Minutes passed then finally, "*Northern Jaeger*, this is Adak. Do you read, over?"

"We hear you, Adak," I responded, my heart racing.

"We will take your injured crewman under the following conditions. First, your vessel will only be allowed two miles offshore from our pier. Second, then the crewman will be met at the pier by an ambulance and taken directly to the airport to an awaiting aircraft that will fly him directly to Anchorage. Do you have the ability to transfer him to shore from that distance, over?"

I glanced over to Tim. He nodded yes. "Roger that, Adak. We have a Zodiac that can bring the patient to the pier, over."

"All right, then, *Northern Jaeger*, you're cleared to proceed. Give us an ETA, and contact us when you're within twenty miles, over."

"Thank you, Adak, we read you. I'll turn you over to our captain for ETA." With that I handed the radio to Tim for him to give them the information they needed. I then thanked Dr. Martin for his help and that ended the call. We immediately pulled our gear and set our course for Adak Island, making full speed ahead.

I might normally set a fractured arm out there, but there are several important things to consider before doing so. One is how badly the bone is displaced from its original position. In a hospital, they have the luxury of x-rays to determine the location of the broken bone to major blood vessels. Blindly moving fractured bones especially with sharp, jagged ends is not a good idea, with the possibility of severing a vein or an artery a real one. Therefore, the decision not to set the bone there was made.

Adak Naval Station was established in 1942 as a staging area for the U.S. military to take back the islands of Attu and Kiska from the Japanese. Then in the 1950s thru the 80s, it was an antisubmarine and surveillance installation against the Soviet Union in the Cold War. By 1994, the base was on the list of bases to be closed as the Soviet Union no longer existed, and its use was no longer needed; but at that time, it hadn't been closed yet, and they took their role in the nation's defense very seriously.

I continued to monitor Peter's condition hourly, concerned mostly with the continued circulation of blood to his lower arm and fingers. For the next thirty-eight hours, I drank a lot of coffee and dozed off for fifteen minutes here and thirty minutes there until we finally reached the outer bay to the entrance of the base.

Peter was able to walk to the Zodiac, his arm securely splinted, and he was lowered without incident in the calm waters of the early morning along with a medical report I had prepared for those who would treat him next. The Zodiac quickly grew smaller and smaller as it sped off to the pier and the waiting ambulance in the distance.

Soon after the Zodiac's return, we were on our way out to sea to continue our pursuit of pollock in the open waters of the Bering Sea. For the next few hours, I'd be asleep in my bunk completely spent from the last several days, content everything had worked out as well as it had.

I was rudely awakened as my body was lifted six inches above my bed and dropped with a thud back into my thin mattress. Lifted up a moment later and dropped again, I knew immediately this was the unmistakable result of sailing into heavy seas. I glanced at my watch as I was lifted and dropped again. I'd been asleep for only three hours.

I rolled over and pulled the covers up over my head determined to ignore my tormentor, only to be lifted up a foot or more off my mattress this time and dumped back into my bunk. At that same moment, an audible dull thud was heard against the side of the ship's hull as it was struck squarely by a large wave, followed by a shattering vibration that went through the entire length of the *Jaeger* from bow to stern. A few seconds later, I could feel the ship begin to list to starboard and continued to list until I was forced to grab hold to the edge of my bunk to keep from being tossed on the floor. OK, I wasn't going to be able to ignore my tormentor. I spent the next several hours lifted, rolled, and dropped on my mattress, settling slowly on being content managing just to stay in my bunk.

After a week's trawling along the western Aleutian Islands, we were full and headed back to Dutch Harbor to off-load, resupply, and head out again. We always had a few crewmen leave and a few arrive. At our time in port, I was happy to see my friend Wayne making his way up the gangway lugging his seabag. Wayne and I had become friends over the years, having made many voyages together. His position on board was as a factory engineer responsible for the maintenance and repair of the seemingly endless array of factory machinery and equipment packed into the processing deck.

He was around my age and lived on the Big Island of Hawaii. He had managed to buy a modest-size piece of land and build a small house upcountry on the side of Mauna Kea volcano. From the ocean floor to its peak, Mauna Kea is the tallest mountain on earth at 33,796 feet, over 13,000 feet from sea level. Wayne lived up high on its slopes, around four thousand feet. It actually got cold there on winter nights, which gave us a few things in common.

I had just bought ten acres outside Homer, Alaska, on a bluff overlooking Kachemak Bay and the Pacific Ocean about a thousand feet in elevation, and I was in the planning stages of moving there and building a place for my growing family. We often spoke of our plans for building and developing our properties. He was a down-to-earth, mellow guy who often stopped by the QC lab to listen to music from our stereo mounted on the lab wall and shoot the breeze.

We soon set sail for yet another voyage, making our way out of the calm confines of Dutch Harbor into the open waters of the Bering Sea. On my last rotation home, I had purchased a then state-of-the-art Sony video recorder. What made this camera unique was it came with a waterproof case that allowed you to record in wet conditions. I was planning on making a home movie of my adventures before I retired from working out there.

As it turned out on this trip, we were sailing directly into a raging storm; and as the day progressed, the sea became increasingly agitated. I was determined to get some storm footage with my new camera. I went to the wheelhouse to discuss my plan with the first mate, Brooks, who I felt would be more open to my idea than Tim. I requested permission to climb the aft net tower to film the storm from the top. Surprisingly he was excited about the idea and agreed to let me do it.

The *Northern Jaeger* had two towers, one aft and one midship, used to pull and set the net and when the net's full, to empty the contents one deck below into the holding tanks located at the stern of the vessel. The towers were about sixty feet high. They had a ladder welded on their side, with a small platform at their tops that were used to maintain the navigation and deck lights mounted there.

By now we were smack in the middle of a fierce gale. The winds registered over seventy knots on the bridge, with the seas averaging twenty—to thirty-five-feet waves routinely leaping over the bow, submerging the front end of the *Jaeger* in a flood of saltwater and spray.

Brooks insisted I wear a Mustang Suit and harness that I could attach to the railing when I reached the top of the tower. He had no problem getting me to agree to that, and preparations were made for my ascent. At the last moment, I decided to wear my arctic parka with a fur-lined snorkel hood for good measure and set off for the aft tower with my camera slung over my shoulder in its protective case.

The deck crew was huddled in the far corner of the trawl deck seeking protection from the incoming waves while mending the huge net used to catch pollock. They all looked up at me as I passed them. Since the sound of the wind and the waves was deafening, I just pointed to myself and then up to the top of the tower and made my way over to the base of the tower. There at the bottom, surrounded by the high bulkheads of the trawl deck, I was relatively protected from the wind and driving sleet.

My heart began to race as I knew, when I had climbed about ten feet up, I'd become fully exposed to the wind's full fury. Some wise shipbuilder back in Germany had welded a cage around the ladder that ran all the way up and allowed just enough room for a man to fit. It did provide some comfort to have the metal cage around me, and I thought it would give me something to grab on to if I did end up falling.

I started my climb, my hands clinching the steel rungs with all my strength. The ship was pitching and listing wildly as I focused my eyes on my hands and the next rung up the ladder and nothing else. This was not just a vertical climb as I found myself holding on for dear life when the ship listed at a forty-five-degree angle out. The reason for the surrounding cage became more than clear as it supported my dangling body as the ladder neared the horizontal position.

Then like a mighty tree swaying in the wind, the tower would begin to move back the other direction until I was on my hands and knees crawling up the ladder at the other end of an inward forty-five-degree list. It was becoming hard to catch my breath due to the hurricane-force wind sucking the air out of my lungs, and I found myself trying to control growing fear as I climbed higher and higher.

I pushed the roaring sound of the wind out of my mind and just focused on my hands clasping each rung tightly as I moved up the ladder. Finally I reached the top and squeezed through the hatch opening to the metal platform. I didn't have the courage to stand up and keep both hands glued to the railing, just summoning enough courage to clip the safety harness I had onto the railing.

As I crouched on the platform, I was beginning to suffocate from the 80 mph winds that sucked the air out of my lungs as they blew past my face. I instinctively reached up with one hand and pulled the snorkel hood I had on my parka to its full-out position, with the hood extended out past my face eight to ten inches. As long as I was looking down or away from the wind, I could catch a breath. Without my parka, I would not have been able to reach or stay on the platform.

The wind was coming straight on bow to stern, the same direction I wanted to film. I couldn't manage to get more than a fleeting glance in that direction without being forced to look away in order to breath. I crouched on the platform. With my head down, tucked into my hood, I could see down to the trawl deck below through the metal grating, seeing the small figures of the deck crew gathered at the bottom of the tower looking up at me. I could feel that I could not stay long exposed there like this, and I began to struggle with one free hand to get my camera swung around off the back of my shoulder so I could get some footage before I'd have to leave.

Finally I pulled the camera around to my chest where I made the necessary adjustments needed to start shooting film. To accomplish this, I was forced to remove my glove. Then still crouching and holding on tightly with one hand, keeping my head and face looking down, tucked as deep as I could be in my hood, I lifted up one hand holding the running camera. I extended my arm up as high as I could in the direction of the bow and pointed the camera hopefully in the right direction and held it there for what seemed like a long time, but it was only about twenty seconds. The temperature was around thirty degrees with an 80 mph wind. I didn't know what the wind chill factor was. The bitter cold instantly froze my hand. Struggling with my frozen-stiff fingers, I managed to secure the camera, tossing it attached to its strap over my right shoulder; and I started down the ladder, the intense fear I was feeling slowly dissipating as I got lower and lower on the swaying tower.

At the bottom, I was met by the deck crew, one of them shouting over the wind, "Are you f—ing crazy?"

I just nodded my head "yes" and pushed my way past them, any attempt at conversation out there being a waste of time. As I reached the wheelhouse, I was thinking I hoped I got some good footage and not just open sky or ocean. I closed the door behind me; back safely in the wheelhouse, I realized how exhausted I was. I could feel the muscles in my arms and hand aching from holding on the ladder and railing so tightly, and I was emotionally spent from the intense mental focus and fear.

"Goddamnit, Doc, you're crazier than a drunken hoot owl. Did you get what you wanted?" Brooks greeted my return.

"Let's see," I said as I pulled the camera from its protective case and rewound the tape cassette inside. After a minute, it was ready to view, and we both pressed in next to each other to view the results on the tiny screen. As we both watched, we could see the bow being lifted and then plunging into the tempest from a bird's eye view, all the while seeing the widely swaying motion of the tower from my position. It was great footage, and I eventually was able to put together an hour-long movie with all the footage I was able to take.

We were in for a hellish week as a powerful low-pressure system was sweeping a wide path across the Bering Sea with hurricane-strength winds and monster seas. Brooks told me about a message sent out from a trawler to our east that had its wheelhouse windows blown in by a rogue wave, forcing it to return to Dutch for repairs. It takes a very large wave to be able to do that as the wheelhouse on large trawlers are at least fifty feet above sea level.

I'd seen seas like this before in the Atlantic as well as the Sea of Okhotsk and knew that no ship was safe while at the mercy of such a storm. I knew each one of us on board quietly said our prayers as we tried to ignore the incredible power raging around us, only to be reminded of our fragile mortality each time the ship listed over on its side and hesitated there as if deciding whether to continue her fight to survive or just give up and let the sea swallow her. A silent collective sigh of relief was released each time the ship slowly righted herself again and again.

This is how a ship takes on a soul and becomes a living thing to those whose lives she holds in her hands. A man can feel a ship struggling, fighting through a terrible storm not only for its own survival but for the survival of her crew and for him personally. And after coming out alive at the other end of a near-death experience, one cannot help but have a real and everlasting affection for what once was an inanimate object but is now a beautiful living entity. It's always been this way and always will be as long as men entrust their lives to the ships they sail in.

The Leg

I couldn't remember a storm of this intensity passing without someone being injured, sometimes seriously. This was to be no exception. As I labored to keep my balance, cursing each time I had to brace myself and hold on to keep from being tossed like a rag doll, I made my way through the factory. While I was taking the readings off various dials, a wide-eyed, frantic factory worker ran up to me, shouting over the perpetual roar of machinery noise. I turned to the side, my head toward his face, straining to hear him yelling over the noise. "It's Wayne, he's hurt bad. Follow me."

My heart jumped a beat as I heard it was Wayne. Factory engineers can be hurt severely as they are always working in and around dangerous machinery with lots of moving parts that are designed to chop, slice, and grind flesh, making no distinction from fish flesh or human.

"Damn it, not Wayne," I muttered as I stumbled to the scene of the accident. It had only been a minute or so since it occurred, and Wayne was still half lying, half sitting in a very awkward position on a fish conveyer belt which was now shut off.

I need to explain here that this conveyer is not the flat-belt type most of us think about when we hear the word "conveyer." These types are all fully constructed of stainless steel and have rows of six steel spikes spaced about eighteen inches apart, running the width of the belt which is about two feet wide. The conveyer is a kind of trough with high sides running along the deck that takes fish to various places around the factory, to be processed. Each spike is twelve inches long, half-inch round, and curved inward in rows, like a pitchfork that moves on a chain drive.

Wayne was working on one of these, standing on it in between the spike rows. The conveyer was shut off and supposed to have a red tag placed on the "on" switch so no one would turn it on while it was being worked on.

Apparently, for whatever reason, someone turned on the conveyer with Wayne standing on it, sending him falling backward and impaling his right thigh on a row of metal spikes. He was sitting in between a spike row with his legs draped over a row of spikes in front of him at his thigh level. When he saw me, he tried to smile. He was as pale as a sheet.

"Hey, Erick, sorry to bother you, my friend," he said.

"Oh, be quiet, Wayne. Damn it, how bad are you hurt?" I replied.

"I'm stuck on these spikes. It hurts like a son of a bitch! I'm going to need some help getting out of here," he explained.

I bent down and looked under his leg to see if I could figure out what the hell was going on. I took my hand and felt under his thigh and could feel a spike running up and disappearing into his flesh. Then I felt along the next spike, and it too was buried deep into his thigh. He had landed on the edge of the row of six spikes, getting impaled on the two outside of the row. I couldn't help but notice that the spikes, like most everything in the factory, were covered as always with the now-familiar thick film of gelatinous fish slime. I knew immediately that this was not good.

I had come straight to Wayne and had not retrieved my trauma bag from the lab yet. I instructed an onlooker to please go get it for me. The lab was only thirty feet away, and the stretcher was in the infirmary. I didn't want to remove his leg from the spikes until I had a way to control the bleeding that would surely occur once they were pulled out and a way to get him out of the factory so I could treat him for shock.

Wayne was dressed in full rain gear and was soaked from working in the wet, cold environment. "Don't go anywhere, Wayne. They'll be right back with my bag."

"Very funny, Doc. Hell, I'm stuck solid."

The spikes had gone through his rain pants, sweatpants, Levi's, and long underwear and were buried up to six inches deep in the muscle on the back of his thigh. Using my trauma scissors, I cut the sleeves of his rain gear and sweatshirt up past his elbow. I carefully inserted a 14-gauge IV needle in his brachial vein and connected it by plastic tube to a liter bag of saline solution.

I placed an oxygen mask over his face and turned on the oxygen. With the stretcher and trauma bag already there, I got a blood pressure reading and heart rate. His blood pressure was strong, so I drew out a measured amount of morphine from a vial and injected that into the portal on the IV line, allowing the narcotic to enter his bloodstream. I then straddled his leg in the standing position, bent over, locked my hands around his thigh, and pulled; then I pulled harder. Slowly I could feel the leg slide up and heard a sickening sucking sound as the spikes came out of his flesh.

Wayne let out a loud scream, "*Aaahhhh!*" and collapsed in the arms of one of the guys supporting him as he sat in the trough. I quickly wrapped thick, heavy trauma dressing around his leg as tightly as I could get it, and we lifted him onto the stretcher and took off for the infirmary one deck up from us.

The weather was horrible; and we were forced to carry him slouched over, so the stretcher was very close to the deck, and had to set him down constantly to keep him and us from being thrown against the narrow hallway bulkheads. When we finally managed to reach the infirmary, we were all exhausted.

I immediately cut off all the layers of pants he was wearing and helped him slip off his coat and shirts. I elevated his legs on pillows. I had Maria, who had been notified of the accident, to hold a pressure dressing over the wounds while I spread out my medical gear on the bed next to him.

I prepared a syringe of lidocaine and a large syringe of saline solution without a needle at its end. I set them next to him on the bunk, tucked in between two pillows to keep them from being dumped on the floor as the ship listed in the heavy seas. I injected the skin around and in the puncture wounds with the numbing lidocaine. I took his vital signs, making small talk as I waited for the medication to numb his leg. All the while, Maria held the dressing firmly in place.

With his wounds numb, I began to flush and irrigate the puncture wounds with saline solution I pushed through the large syringe. I inserted the syringe into the puncture sites as deeply as I could get it and pushed down hard on the syringe's plunger. I needed to get all the way to the deepest part of the puncture wounds and make every effort to flush out any remnants of fish slime as I could, or Wayne would be in serious trouble; as always, the onset of infection was my main concern.

After several minutes and two liters of saline solution, I felt confident I'd cleaned the wound well enough. Wayne was moaning and complaining of intense pain from his injury. I decided to start him on some Vicodin orally for his pain and finished wrapping a clean trauma pad over his open wounds. With Maria staying with Wayne, I went to the ship's office to get off a fax to Dr. Martin in Seattle with a report and request for further treatment.

Dr. Martin was concerned about the almost-certain onset of an infection. I was instructed to begin an antibiotic drip through the IV line I'd started, and he would work on getting a transfer underway on his end as I should do on my end as well. I returned and started the antibiotics running then set out for the wheelhouse.

Tim was on duty, and when I explained the situation, he informed me that the weather was not expected to let up for at least a week.

Until then, there would be no sea or airlift for Wayne, and I was on my own until further notice.

"Do what you have to do, Doc, to keep Wayne stabilized. Do you think you can manage it?" he asked.

"We'll find out soon enough. I'll do the best I can," I replied and returned to the infirmary.

I could take care of Wayne in his own room and had him moved there. From experience, I knew to draw a line around the wound's red area with a black marker. I made plans to have Wayne soak in a tub of warm water and Epsom salt at least once a day and started him on an oral regime of antibiotics and pain meds. With that my day was over, and I eagerly ate and went right to bed not knowing what or when I'd be called upon next.

Six hours later, I awoke, dressed, and went to Wayne's room anxious to check on his condition. He was sacked out in a deep sleep from the pain meds he was on. I woke him and removed his dressing to get a look at his wounds. I was disappointed to find that the skin surrounding the puncture wounds was a shiny, bright, flaming red color and had expanded several inches past the black marker outline I'd drawn the day before around what was then the perimeter of redness.

The puncture sites were swollen and clearly showing signs of infection. I realized I had to go into emergency mode and aggressively treat his wounds if I had any chance of getting control of the potentially maiming or even fatal infection that was now attacking his body.

I prepared a syringe filled with hydrogen peroxide without a needle on the end and numbed the inflamed openings of his wounds with injections of lidocaine. His wounds resembled bullet holes. By squeezing the skin on the back of his thigh, I was able to get the puncture openings to open into perfectly round holes, a half-inch round, six inches deep, and fill each one with the peroxide solution. After letting the wounds bubble and foam for several minutes filled with peroxide, I soaked up the solution with a thick gauze pad.

Next I had a fish tote brought in from the factory. These were made of a thick, heavy-duty, grey plastic. Their dimensions were approximately four feet long, three feet wide, and two and a half feet high. In the shower in his room's bathroom, I cleaned the tote with hot water soap and hydrogen peroxide and then filled it with warm water and a liberal dose of Epsom salt. I then helped Wayne over to the tote and, cradling him in my arms, lifted him gently into the tub where Wayne could soak his leg in the heavy salt solution.

All the while, we struggled to keep our balance as the seas outside the ship continued to pound the vessel without letup. With the tub in the shower basin, it was of no concern as the water in the makeshift bathtub sloshed out over the rim of the tote, and it was easy to keep it filled with the showerhead over us. Due to the miracle of osmosis, you could see pus and blood being drawn out of the wounds in long, stringlike strands. This was good, and it was the effect I was looking for. After a half hour soaking and sloshing in the tote, I carried him back over to his bunk.

We would continue this routine every six hours around the clock. After the first day and four treatments, I could see the redness and swelling retreating; extremely relieved, I continued the treatment with renewed enthusiasm. Several days later, all the redness and swelling were gone as well as the pain it caused Wayne. I was able to wean him off the powerful pain medication, and his energy level improved by the hour. I allowed his wounds to air out and kept them undressed as much as possible. They began to dry out and heal quickly with each passing day.

After eight long days, I was notified by Captain Tim that the storm was passing, and he had made arrangements to have Wayne transferred to an inbound trawler for Dutch Harbor and a flight to a hospital in Anchorage.

The next day, we transferred Wayne off the *Northern Jaeger.* By now he had made a remarkable recovery from his serious injuries, and we had become close friends in the process, no surprise after spending so much time caring for him. He was extremely grateful for all I had done for him, and I was extremely relieved that I was able to keep a potentially serious injury under control, given the unique circumstances we were faced with.

I wouldn't see old Wayne again for another six months when I was heading home for what was to be my last voyage on the *Northern Jaeger* and he was just arriving to set sail on her for another trip. On the pier where I met up with him, he explained how, when he got to the hospital in Anchorage, the doctor and staff were amazed at his condition and asked who had been treating him all that time out in the middle of the Bering Sea. Impressed with the care he had received at sea, they told him his wounds were well on their way to a complete healing, and there was nothing more for them to do at the hospital.

He was released an hour later and allowed to fly home to Hawaii. He insisted I give him my home address; and after several hugs and a flurry of handshakes, we tearfully wished each other the best and went on our separate ways, never to see each other again.

Trawler men have the hearts of lions.

—Allen Villiers

Chapter 19

End of an Era 1996

The end came suddenly. After eighty-one days at sea, I returned to Anchorage in late May, amazed to see the stunning changes in the seasons that had taken place since I'd left. There had been three feet of snow on the ground with the temperature hovering around zero when I left. Now the countryside was an explosion of lush green, wildflowers, warmth, and bright daylight from a crystal-clear subarctic sun. My beautiful wife had picked me up from the airport. She was seven months pregnant with our first child. As we drove home, I marveled at the explosion of life that had burst from the long-frozen landscape; I was sensitive to all the colors from the trees and spring flowers after being so long at sea.

I had never made plans for the time I would not go to sea again. In the back of my mind, I knew the time was coming and had just let it ride when the decision would be made to stay home would come. My wife and I had rented a small house in Anchorage with a fenced-in yard. We had worked hard the summer before to turn most of the yard into a lush garden full of flowers and vegetables.

It was just the time of year to plant that year's crop; with the daylight hours this far north approaching nineteen hours and temps in the seventies; anything planted in the rich earth grew with a speed and intensity that was stunning. We were eager to start planting and spend time outdoors after a long cold winter.

The economy in Alaska was booming, and the young city of Anchorage was growing as fast as the fireweed that sprang up along the roads and fields. There were a lot of construction jobs that paid high wages, so I called a former boss of mine to see what the prospects of employment were in town. I was a journeyman insulator from years ago. They paid $35 an hour for experienced insulators there in Alaska. My boss was delighted to hear from me and explained that there was plenty of full-time work available, and he was in need of all the experienced journeymen he could find. I told him I'd think about it and get back to him soon.

The timing of my son's birth was right around the time I'd be heading back out to sea. My wife and I had long ago decided that I'd be around to assist in giving birth to our child. It was quickly becoming clear that I wasn't going to make the next voyage. I called the office in Seattle to let my QC supervisor know I would not be able to make the next trip I was scheduled for.

There had always been some contention between me and the Quality Control Department at Oceantrawl because of my dual work responsibilities on the boat. I had always let them know that my job as a medic came first for me, even as I had moved my way up to a supervisor in the QC lab on the *Northern Jaeger*. My medic responsibilities had, over time, come in conflict with my lab responsibilities while at sea, with the other QC techs filling in for me when I was attending to patients.

At first this was taken in stride, but as time went on, there had become more and more pressure for me to put my medical work aside and take my work in the lab more seriously. This I had always resisted, and after a while this was seen as having a bad attitude toward the QC lab. Of course, I didn't have a bad attitude toward the lab. It was just that I was a medic first that also worked in the lab, not the other way around.

The differences between the lab and myself had been building for years. So when I called my supervisor in Seattle and explained how I'd like to skip the next voyage so I could be home for my child's birth, I was a little taken aback when she told me if I wanted to stay home, I'd be terminated from my position in the lab. As far as my job as a medic on the *Jaeger* was concerned, she had no control over that, but I'd no doubt have to work as a factory worker from then on if I didn't work in the lab.

Upon hearing this, along with her somewhat snotty attitude, there was a moment of silence while my mind raced through the meaning of what she had just said. Then in a calm and matter-of-fact tone, I told her that I'd no longer be working for Oceantrawl and hung up.

I had been working at sea already for five years. It had become a part of me. My mind reeled with thoughts of doubt and uncertainty on whether I'd made the right decision. I sat down in the living room gathering my thoughts about how I'd tell my wife. I looked over and saw her outside, through the window, tending our garden in the afternoon sun, straining to reach the ground over her pregnant belly.

I felt a smile spreading across my face as I let go of any thoughts of the past and began to think of our future. My time on the Bering

Sea had transformed me in profound ways. I began to feel as if those experiences I had there were a gateway to the next level of my life. As I gazed lovingly at my wife moving gently through the garden, the Bering Sea began to release its mysterious grip on me.

I stood up and went over to the window, tapping on it until I got my wife's attention and motioned her to come inside. I felt my heart begin to beat a little faster a moment. Later she came into the room. "What is it, sweetheart?" she asked softly.

"I have some good news. I'm not going to sea anymore. I quit my job with Oceantrawl."

She immediately came over to me, and we embraced.

"I'm so happy," she said. Then sensing how I might be feeling, she asked, "Are you going to be all right, not going back? I know how much it means to you."

A soft cool breeze blew in from the open door, bringing with it the fragrance of blooming spring wildflowers. I could hear the laughter from the neighbor's kids as they played in the yard next door. "Yeah, I'll be fine," I answered her. "I'm home now."

Epilogue

After returning from the Sea of Okhotsk on the *Royal Enterprise*, I received a call one day from the office of Arctic Ice Fisheries. It seemed that after four months sailing around on the *Arctic Surveyor*, Justin had made his way back to Seattle. He promptly hired a lawyer and sued Arctic Ice Inc. for his pay and pain and suffering inflicted on him by the captain and crew of the *Royal Enterprise* during our voyage to Kamchatka.

The president of Arctic Ice Inc. asked me if I'd come in and give my side of the story of events that occurred at sea as I was seen as a neutral member of the crew. At first I was insistent about not wanting to have anything to do with testifying against the crew of the *Royal Enterprise* because I might come across one or several of them in future trips to Dutch Harbor and did not want to end up unconscious in an alley behind some bar. However, after some thought on the matter, I did decide to come in and give my side of the story with the condition that my name would never be linked to any of the information attained in the hearings; they agreed to this.

This turned out to be an interesting experience. I arrived at downtown Seattle one grey, drizzly day and made my way by elevator to the top of a tall skyscraper. As I exited the elevator, I was struck by the opulence of the surroundings. I had never seen the office of a CEO of a large corporation. It was luxurious, with lush carpeting and incredible paintings on the walls. There was a huge conference table made of some kind of exotic wood, which was stunning, beautifully trimmed in gold inlay, and with large, plush leather-bound chairs.

I was seated at the table with a lawyer and the president and vice president of Arctic Ice Inc. There I gave my deposition. With the help of the information I gave, Justin was able to receive his pay for his hellish voyage and some extra for pain and suffering, the money coming out of the captain and the rest of the crew's wages. I never did run into any of the crew of the *Royal Enterprise* again.

A year after Mac was hospitalized with hepatitis A, he returned to the *Northern Jaeger* much to my delight. I had missed the old son of a gun and had worried about him often. Upon his return, he told me of his ordeal to recovery. There isn't a cure for hepatitis; the only treatment is to try and strengthen the immune system of the infected person so it can fight off the virus and put it into submission. Mac was fortunate he was young and healthy without any other medical condition that could have made his recovery impossible. He told me of many months of intense illness followed by many more months of weakness and difficulty getting around. Finally he began to regain his strength and was able to return to the *Northern Jaeger*, where he worked for many years after his recovery.

Josh, who was airlifted off the *Northern Jaeger* with a serious heart condition, spent a week in intensive care and was lucky to survive. He was never allowed to return to sea, and eventually he found a good job on land, where he works to this day.

For several years, after I last saw Wayne on the pier at Dutch Harbor, I received Christmas cards from him, expressing his eternal thanks for my care of him, always followed by an open invitation to come to Hawaii and stay with him as long as I wanted.

Remember Henry? He stayed the entire voyage working with his injury. I ran into him in Alaska five years after I retired, on the bank of a river one summer while salmon fishing; and ten years after that, in 2009, while walking with a friend on a trail in Anchorage. Talking to her about Henry, I looked up and saw him walking toward me with his girlfriend. He showed me his finger and hand, the scars still plainly visible. We hugged and shook hands, thrilled to see each other again after so long.

The *Northern Jaeger* still sails the Bering Sea on regular trips from Dutch Harbor although Oceantrawl Inc. no longer exists. The three trawlers *Northern Jaeger*, *Hawk*, and *Eagle* were sold to American Seafoods Inc. Captain Tim is still captain of the *Northern Jaeger* and is known for being one of the best in his field.

Oh yeah, remember Gary, way back from chapter one? I did see him again, sailing with him on several more voyages over the years. He told me of his trip to the hospital and how they marveled at his care and fancy stitchwork on his face. He was released an hour after arrival as there was nothing else for them to do as I had done all that was possible. As he spoke, I looked closely for any sign of scarring on his face and was satisfied that unless you looked very closely and knew what you were looking for, the scar was almost invisible. Gary was very thankful, and I was really pleased as well.

It's been fourteen years since my last voyage. I'm already in my fifties. As the years have passed, I've come to realize how significant my time at sea was. We've all heard of or read about those coming-of-age rituals practiced by so-called primitive tribes around the world, where they create profound and peak experiences to mark the moment when a person comes of age.

In New Guinea, young men are held by a length of twisted vine tied to their ankles and jump off hundred-foot towers hoping to cheat death by just touching their heads lightly on the ground. In Australia, members of the tribe go on a walkabout, spending weeks isolated and alone in a vast wilderness. In the Amazon, boys put on gloves woven out of vines and filled with stinging fire ants, enduring searing pain to prove their manhood.

Stronger, more confident, grounded, and sure of myself and my purpose, it's become clear to me how I was subconsciously searching for my own rite of passage, how my experiences on the Bering Sea propelled me toward manhood. Some men find themselves as they jump from a tower held only by a vine around their ankle, others wandering alone for days in an endless wilderness; for me, it was straining to keep from being washed overboard from the deck of a ship, beyond the northern horizon.

The End

Dedication

This book would be incomplete without the honorable mention of the United States Coast Guard. They have a naval and air station on Kodiak Island where they fly dozens of extraordinary and extremely hazardous missions to rescue fishermen and seamen in the Bering Sea every year. These highly trained and brave men and women continually risk their lives so others may live and saves dozens of people lives every year. They are true heroes.

About the Author

I have two beautiful children, a son and a daughter. I have worked on oil rigs on Alaska's Arctic coast, commercial diving vessels in Prince William Sound, and construction sites from Barrow to Valdez, Alaska, and many points in between. I'm currently living in Anchorage, Alaska, attending college to earn a Bachelor of Science degree in construction management; and I have a small business where I make handmade rustic furniture and I also work in the residential construction trades part-time.

In the future, I plan on owning my own construction company, building homes made out of renewable and recycled materials, and perhaps I may write another book.

Edwards Brothers,Inc!
Thorofare, NJ 08086
21 May, 2010
BA2010141